THIS BOOK BELONGS TO

....

....

....

....

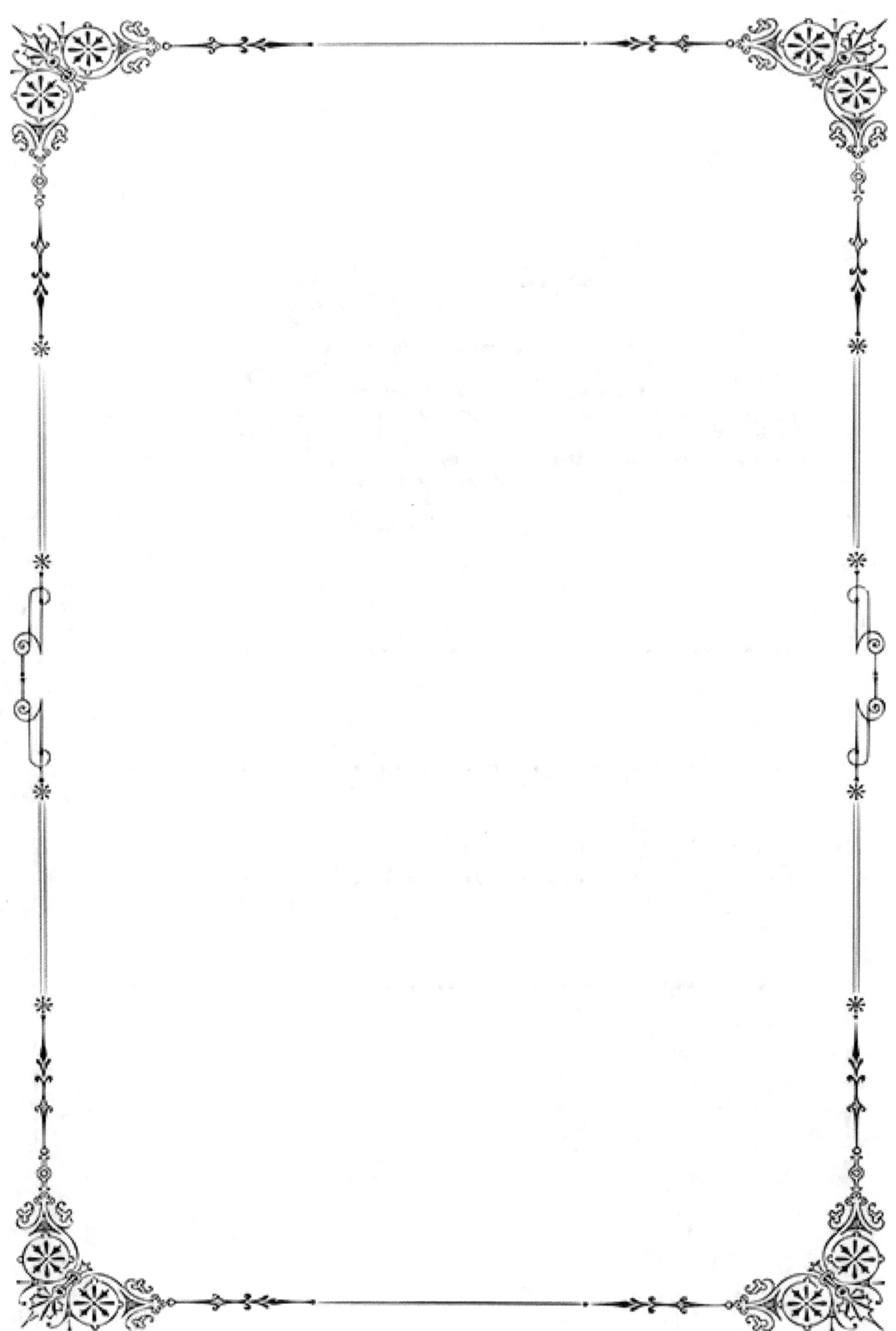

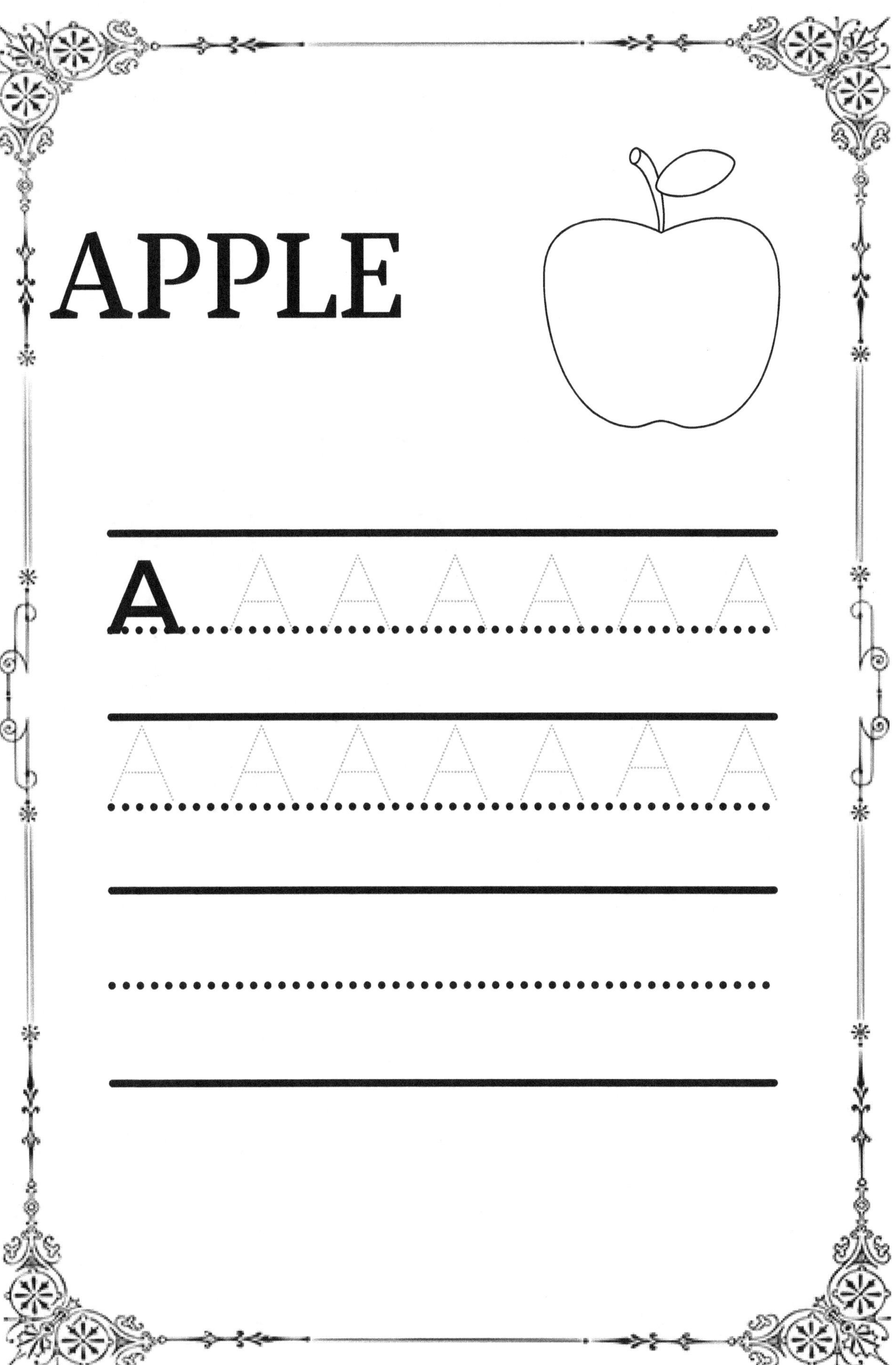

APPLE
A

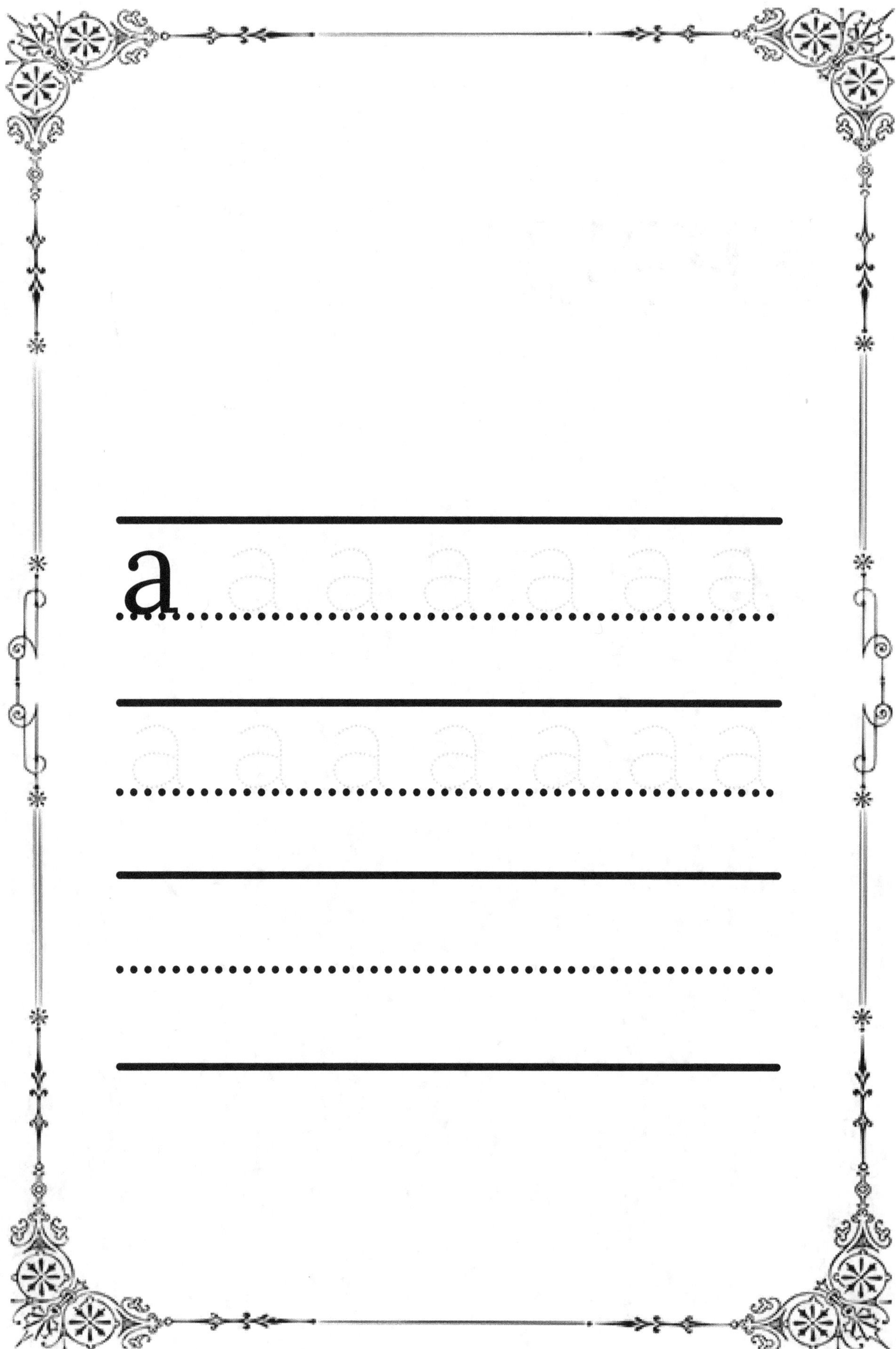

a a a a a a a
a a a a a a a

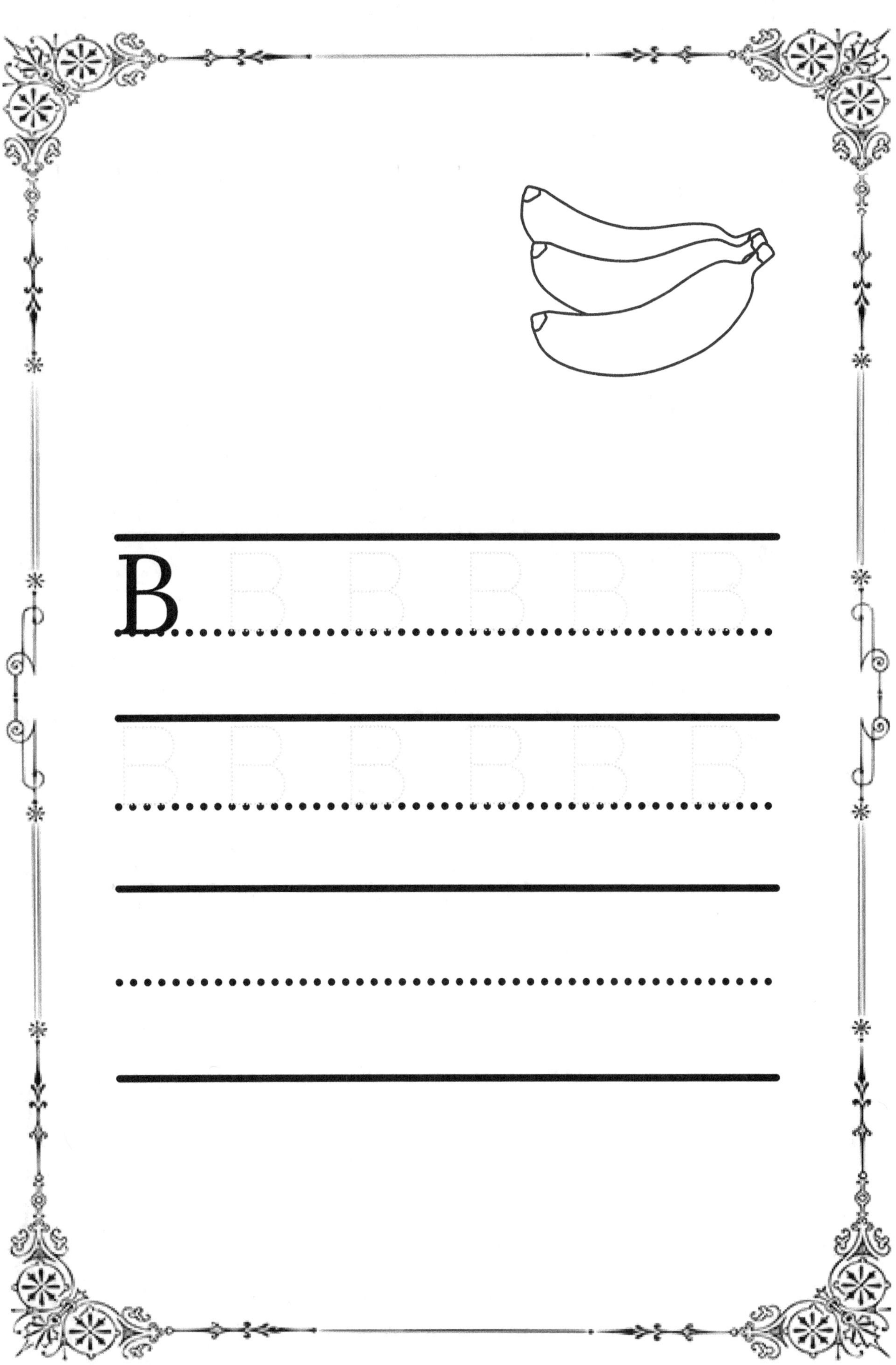

B

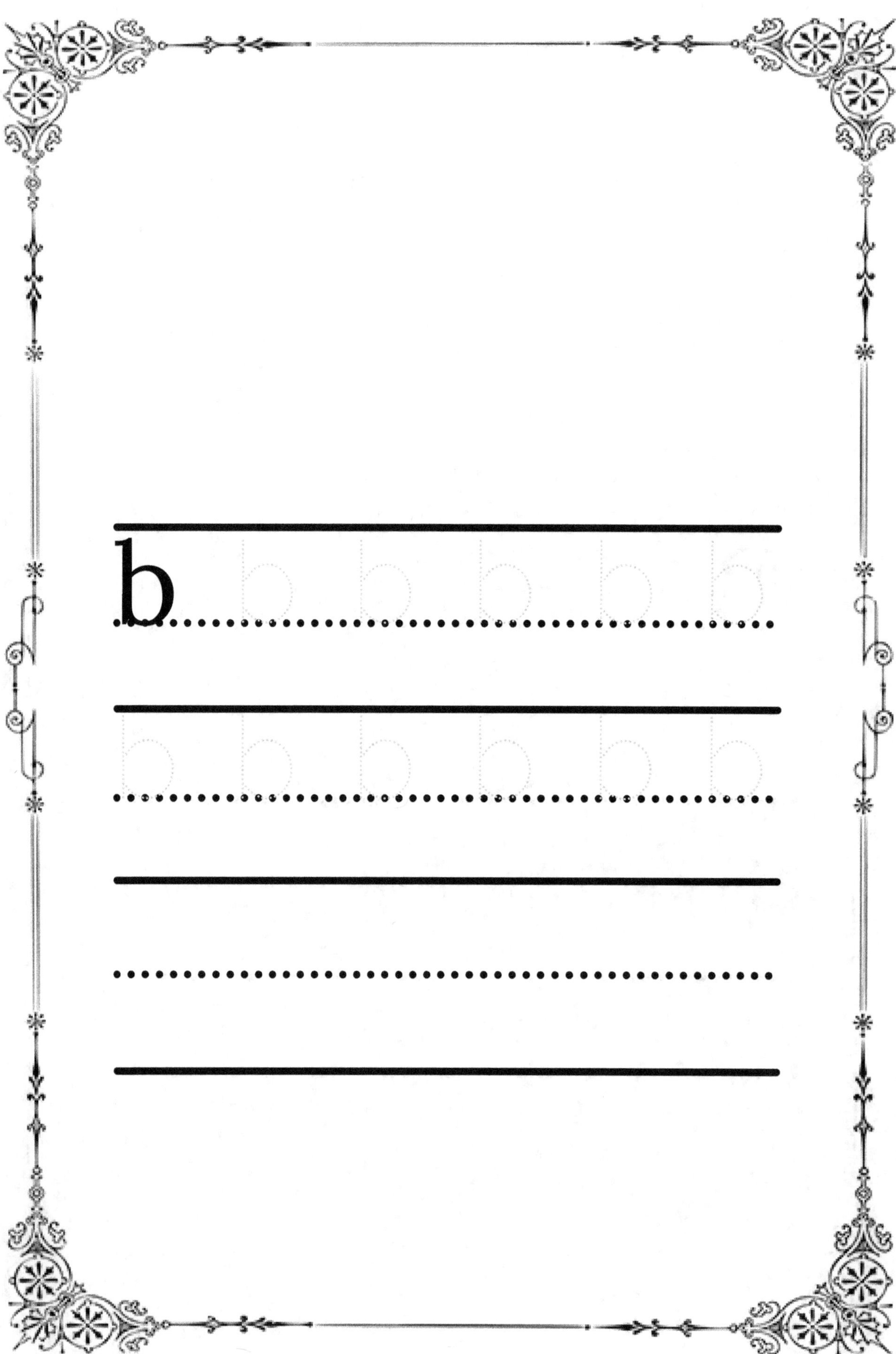

CAMEL

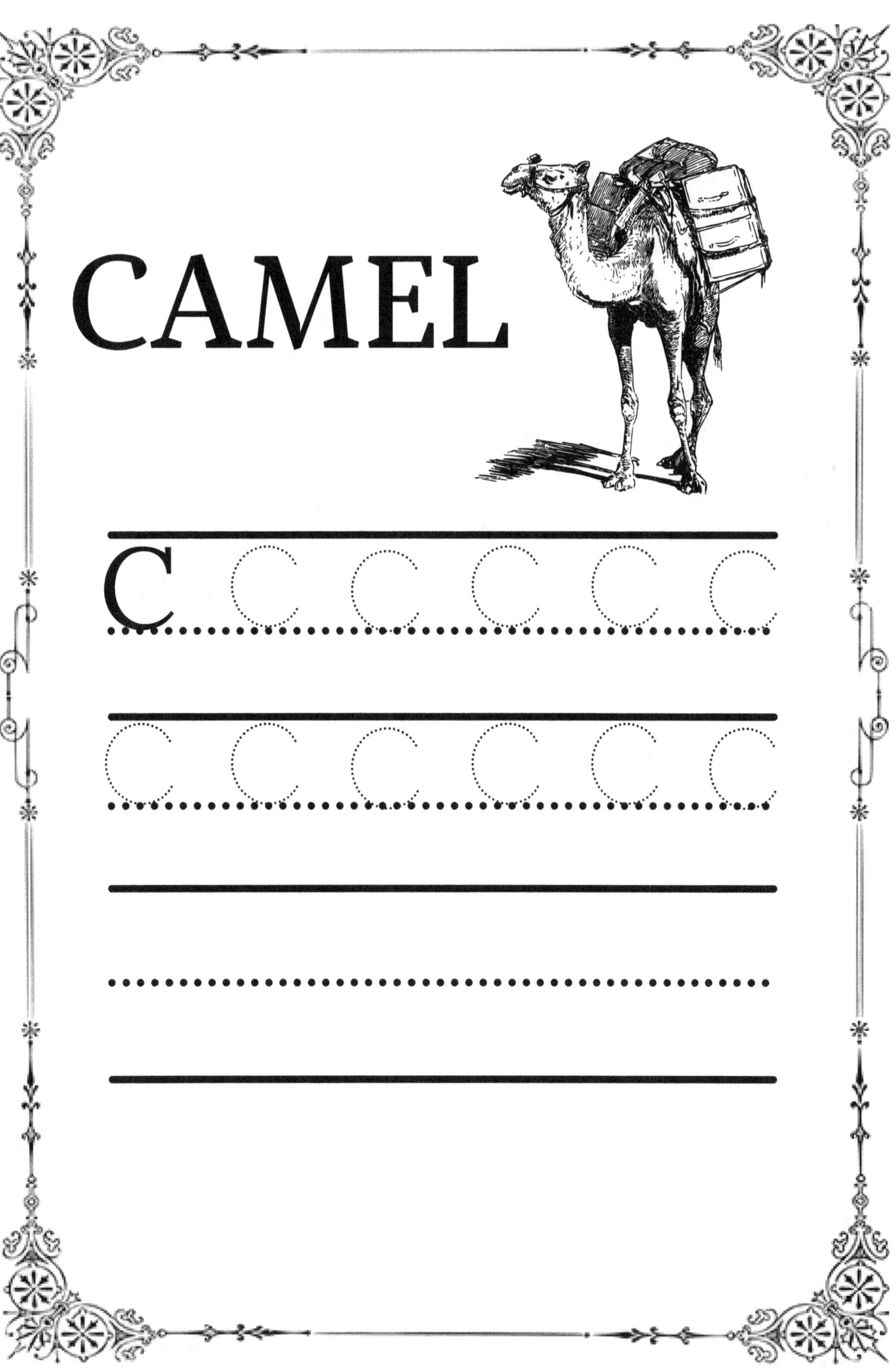

C

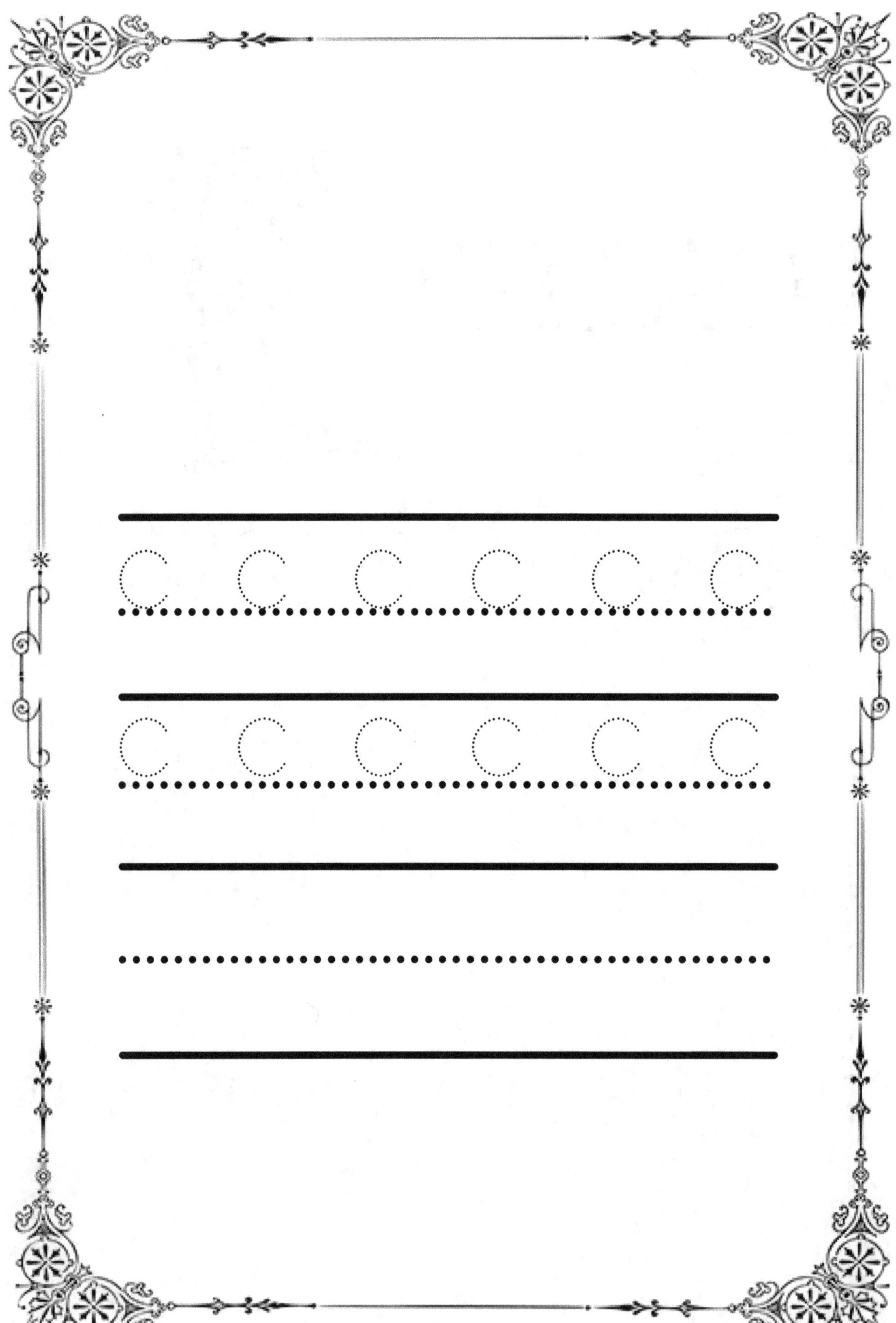

DOG

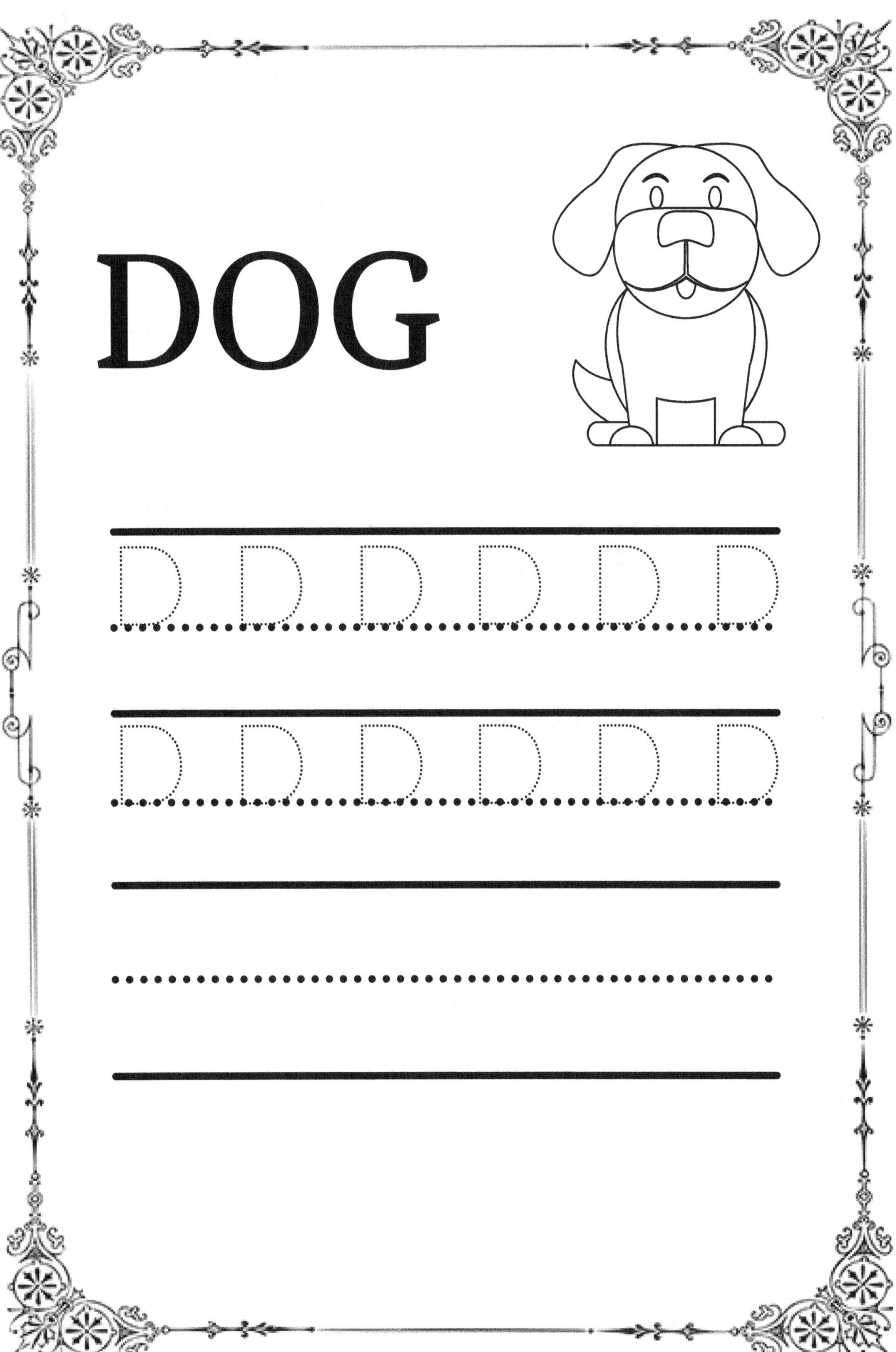

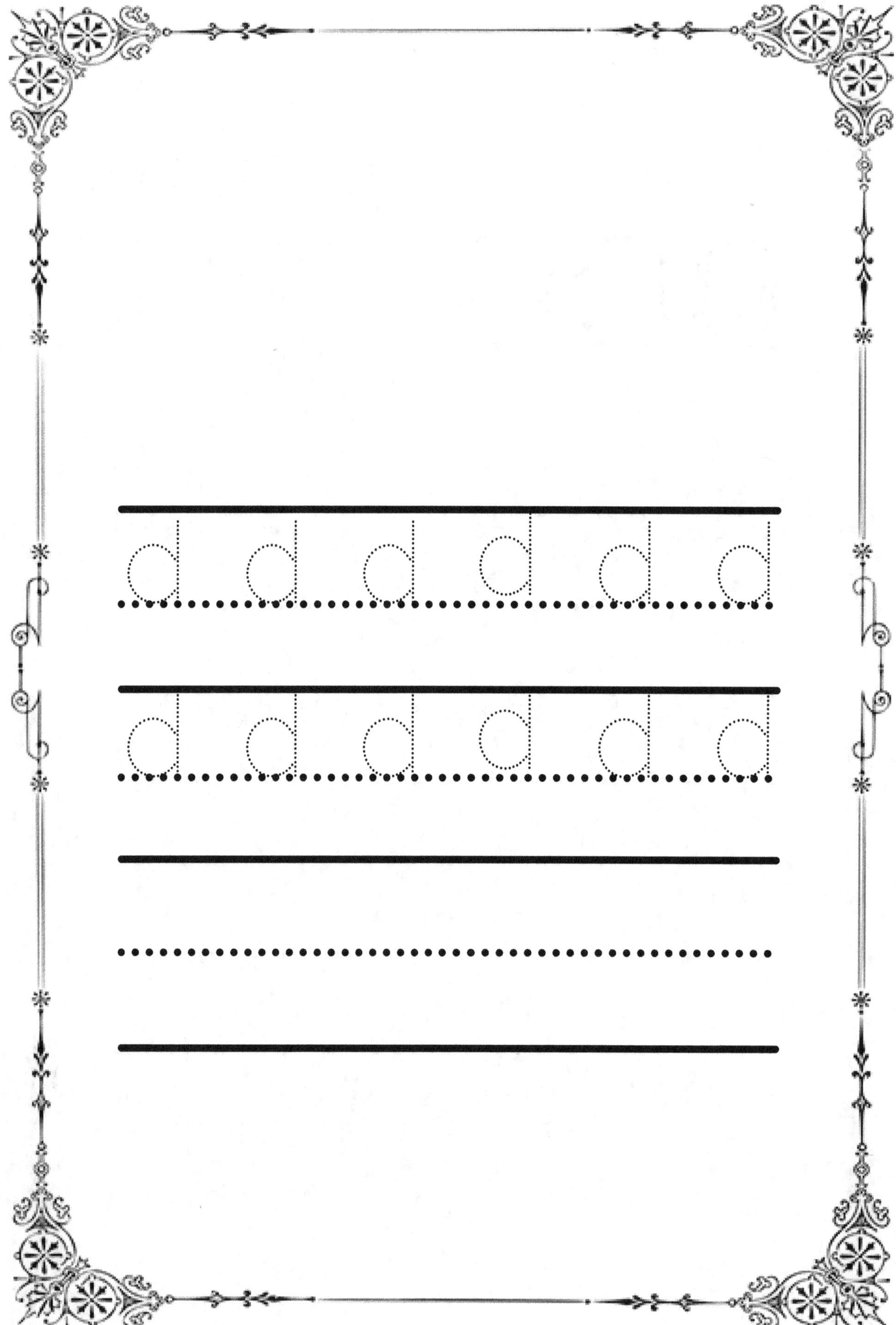

Elephants

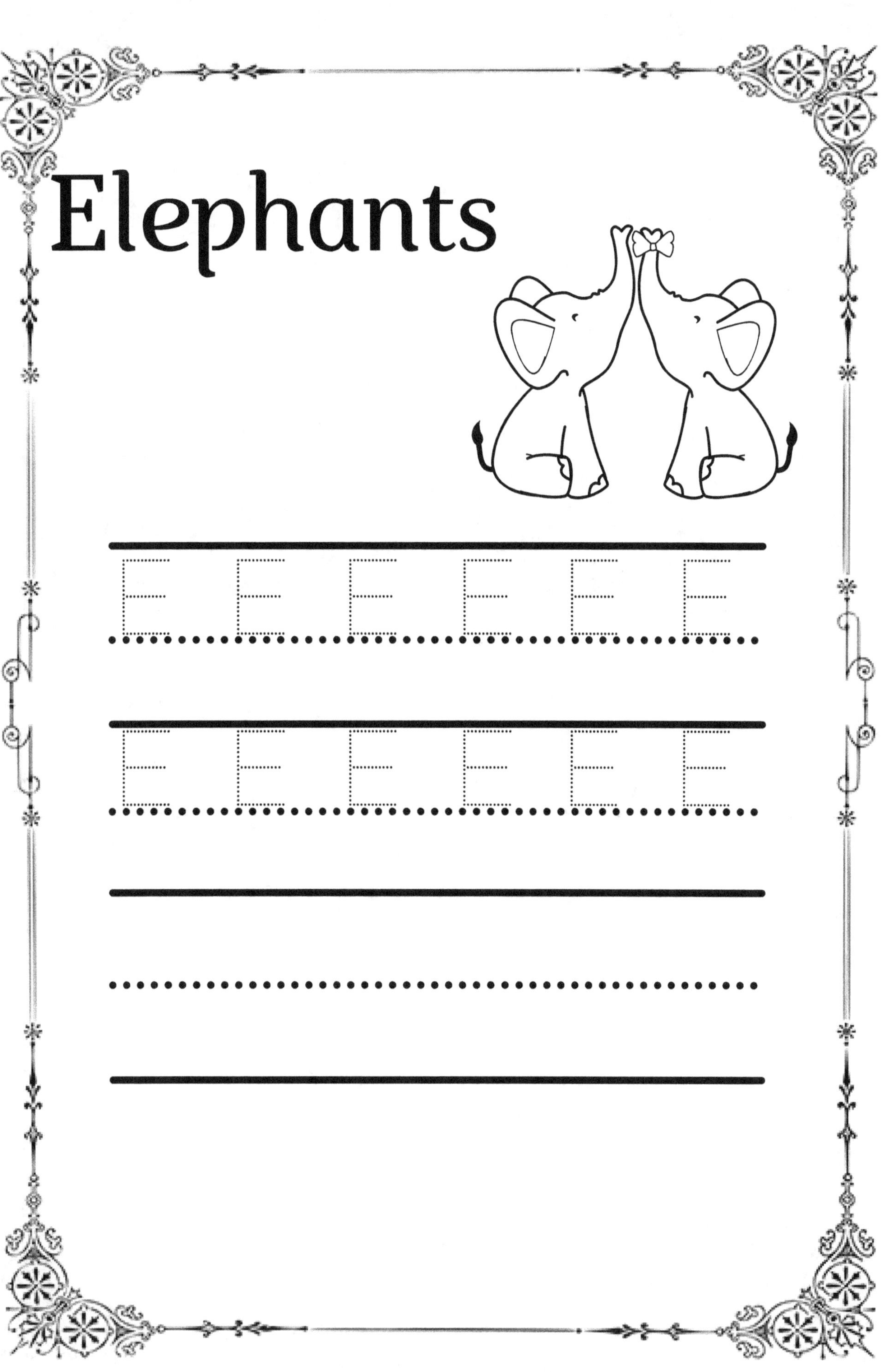

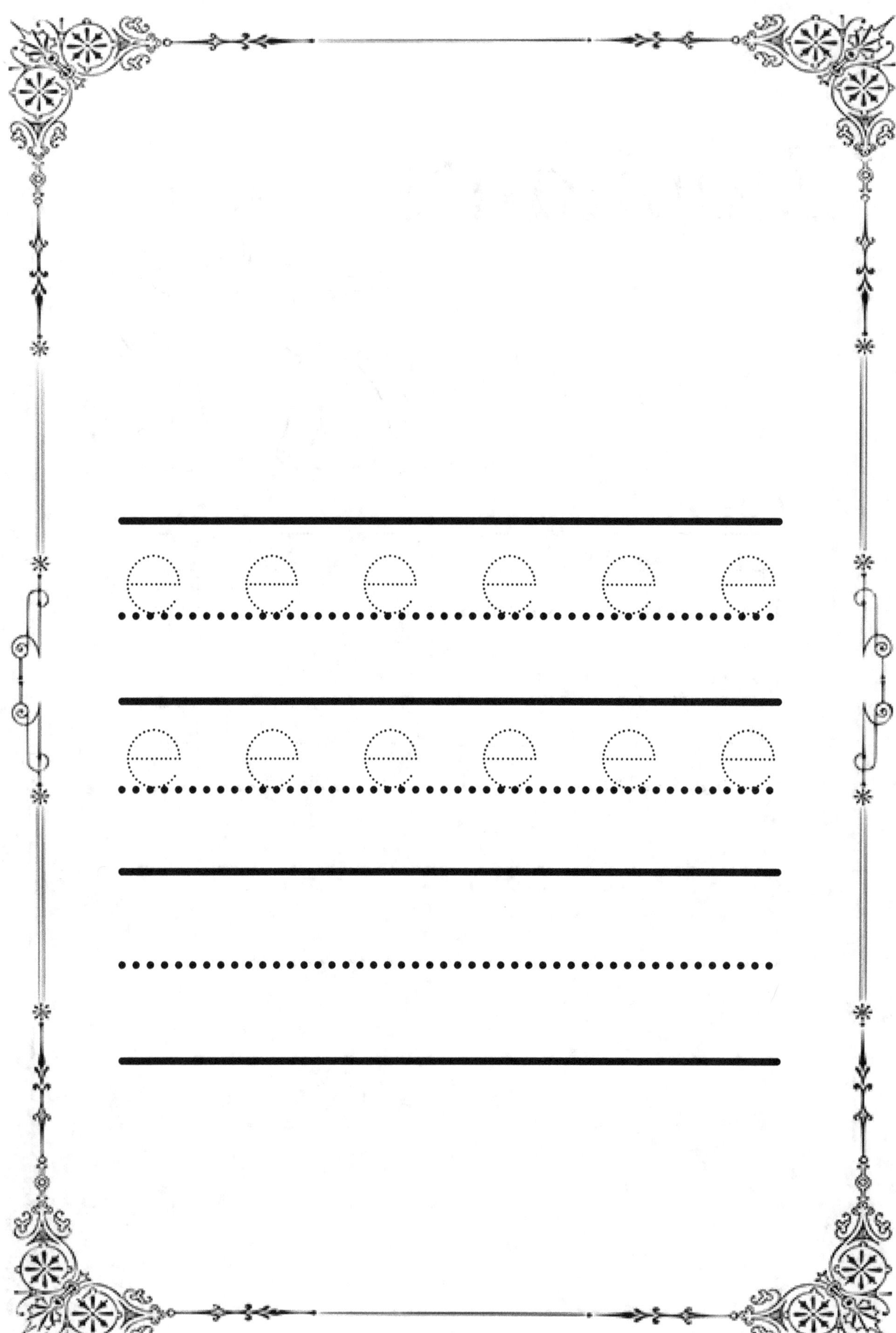

Frog

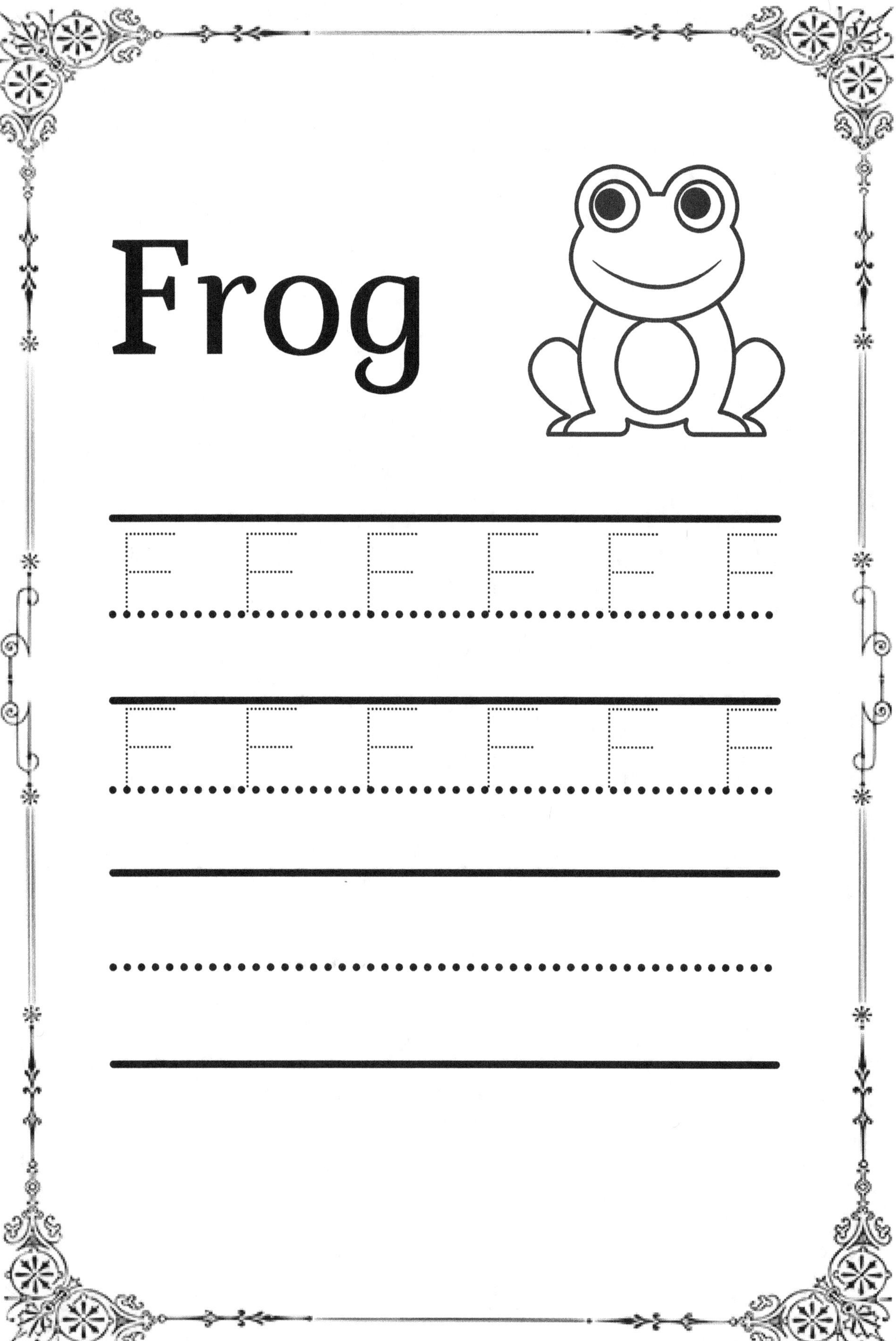

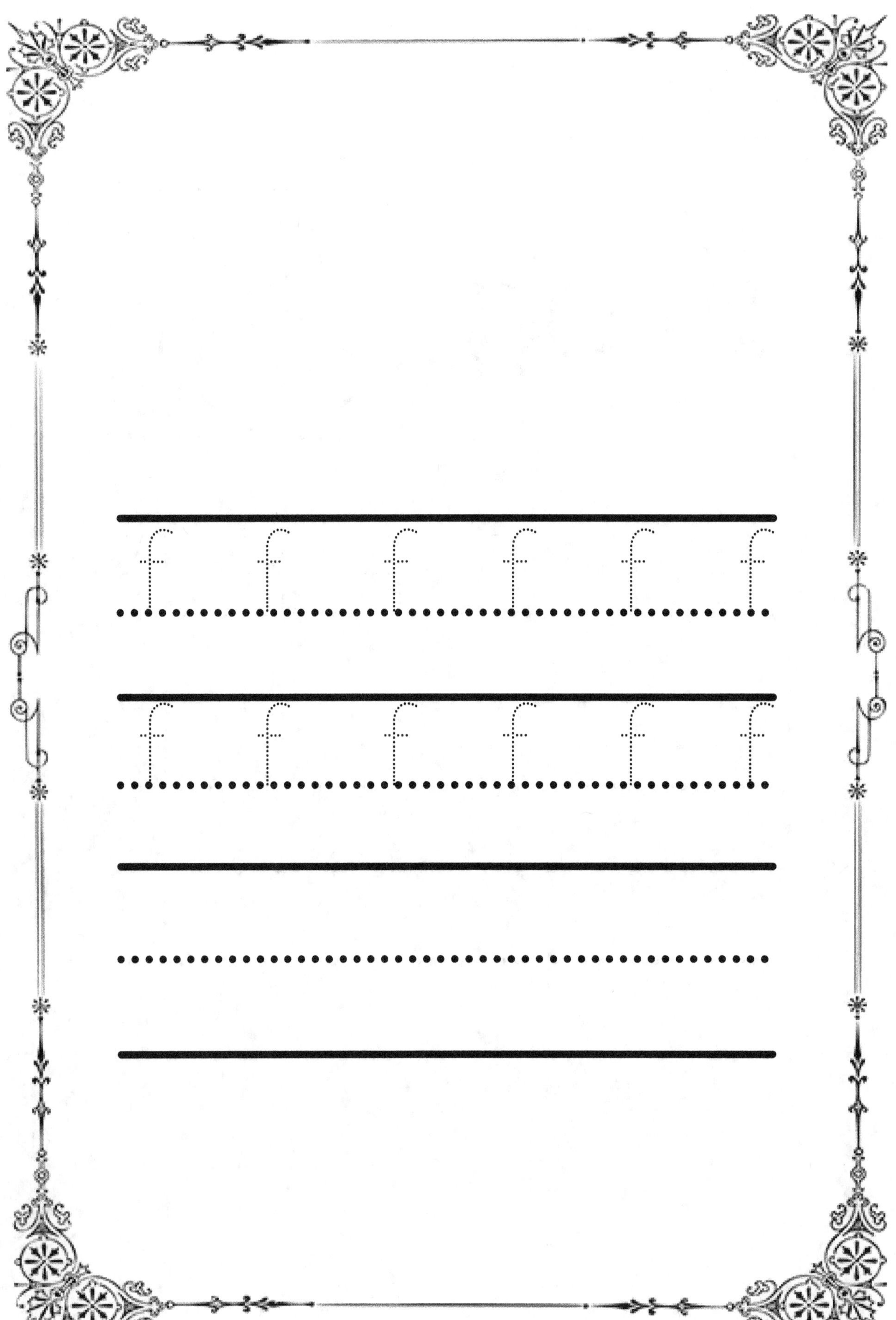

f f f f f f
f f f f f f

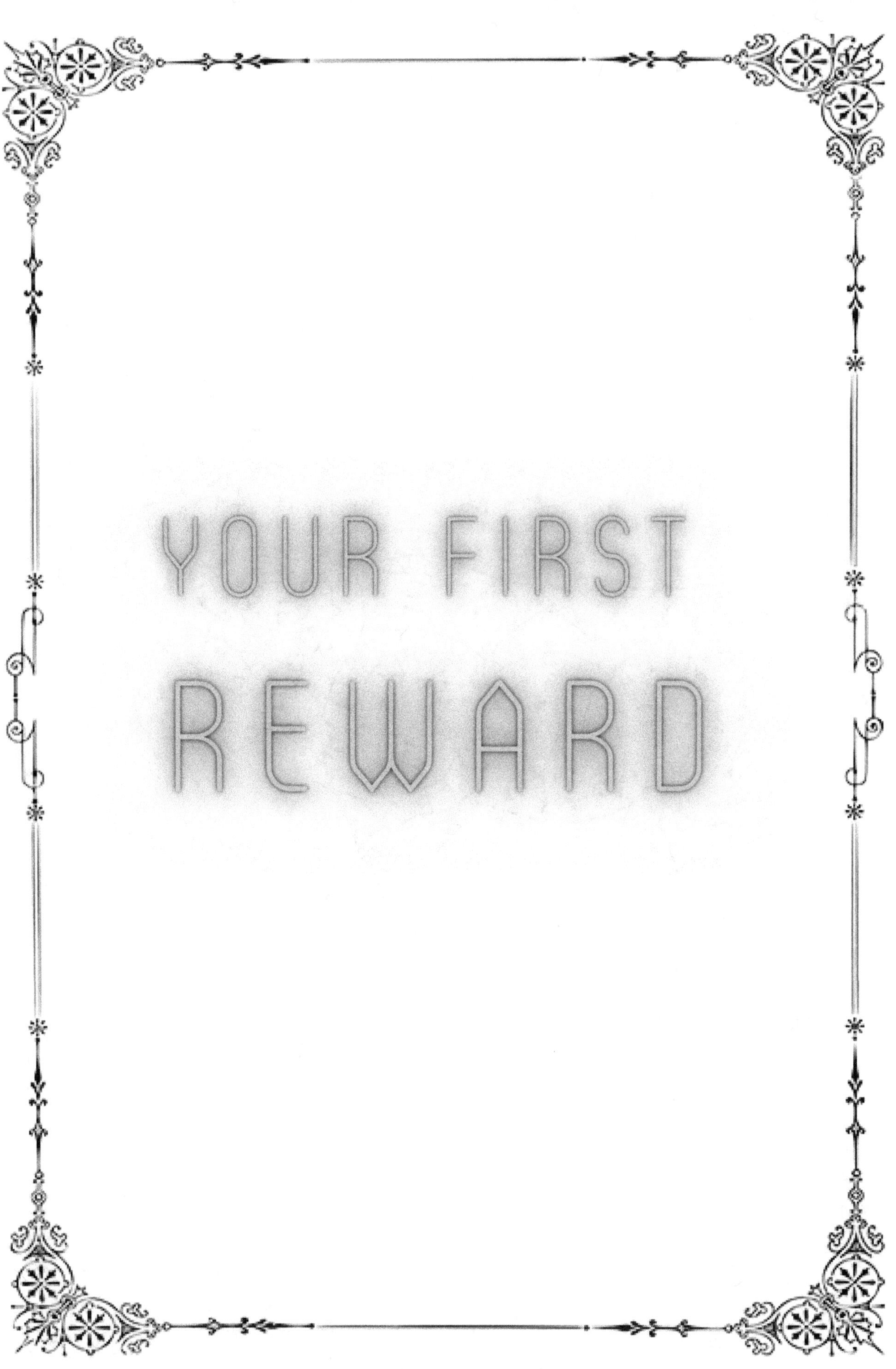

YOUR FIRST
REWARD

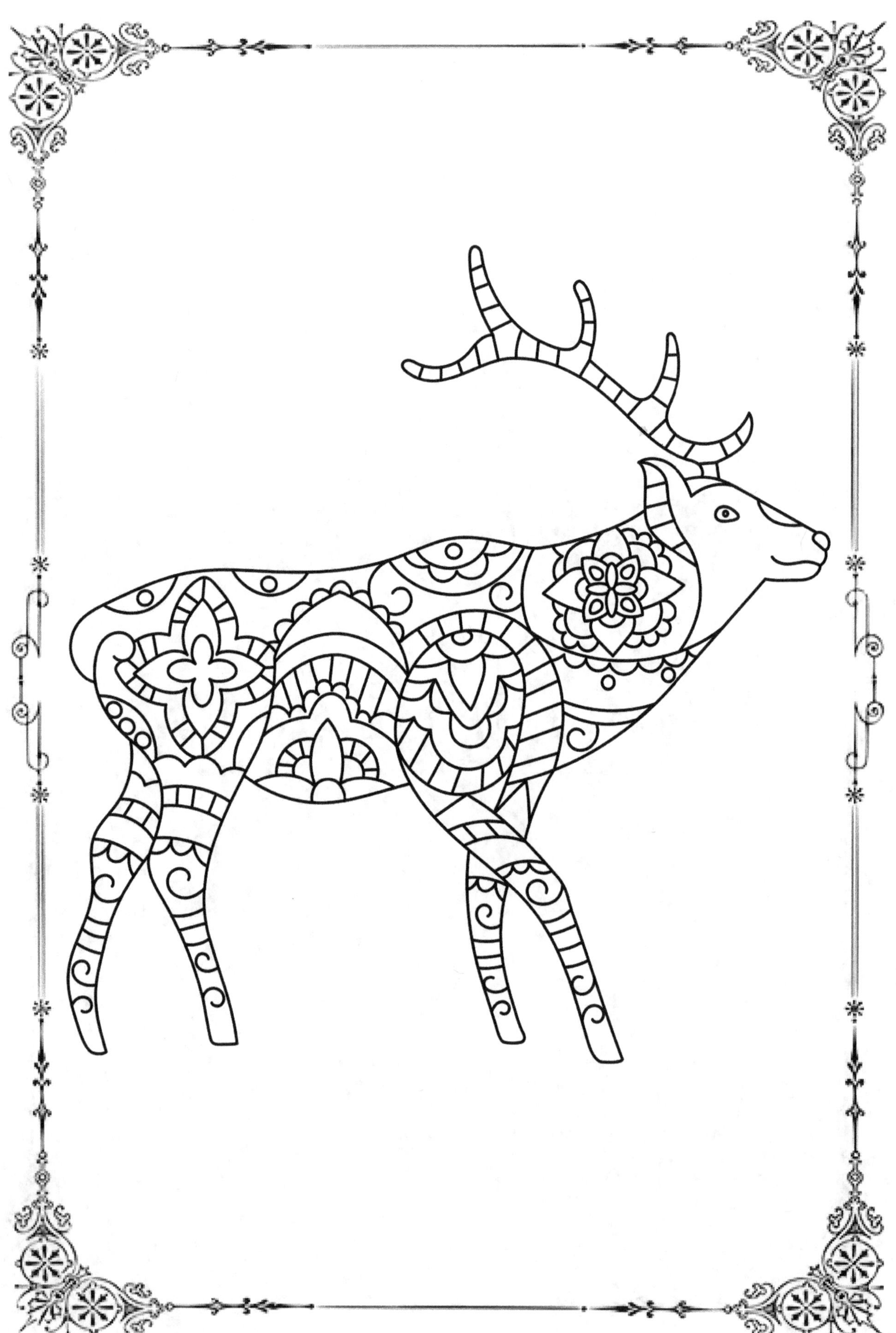

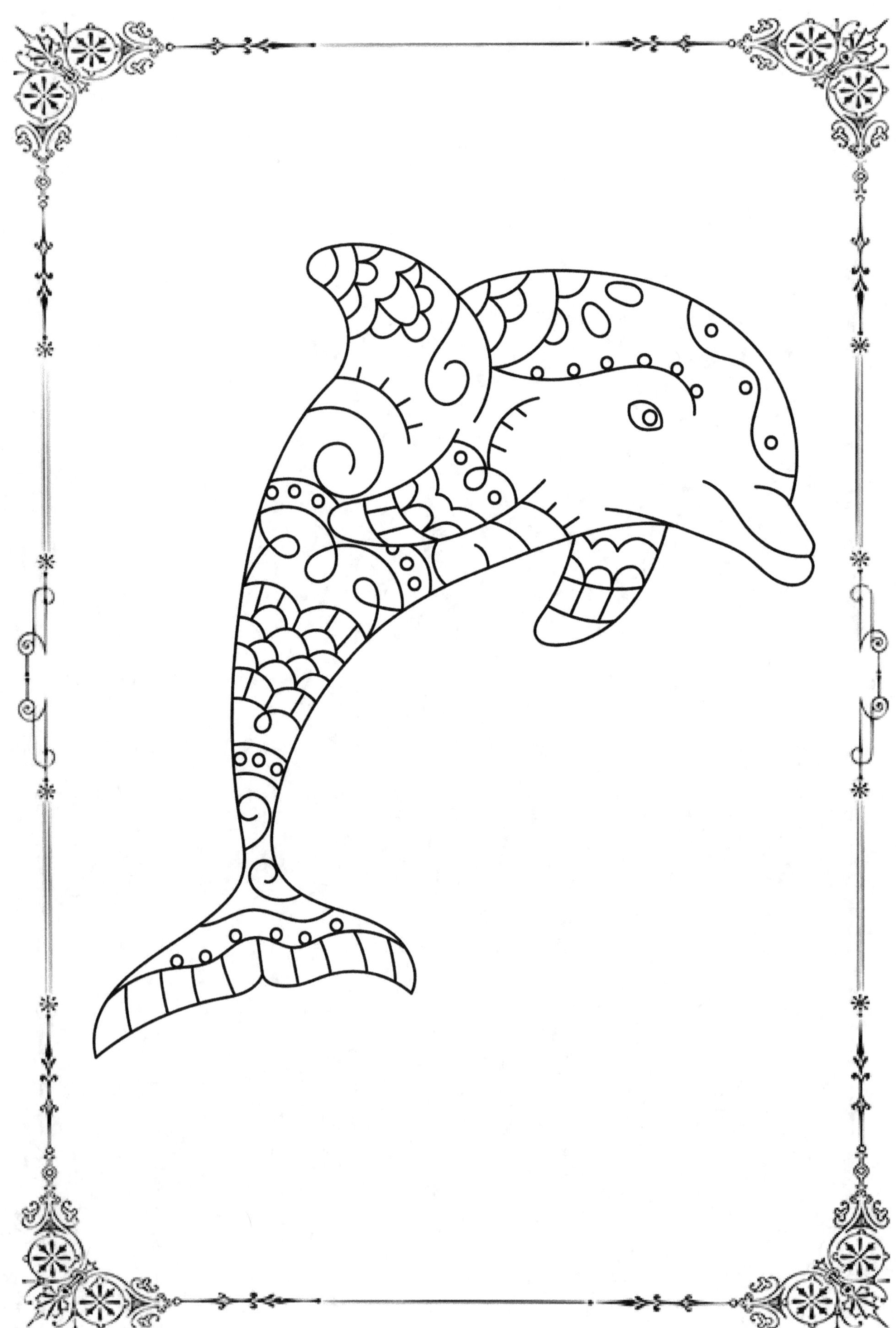

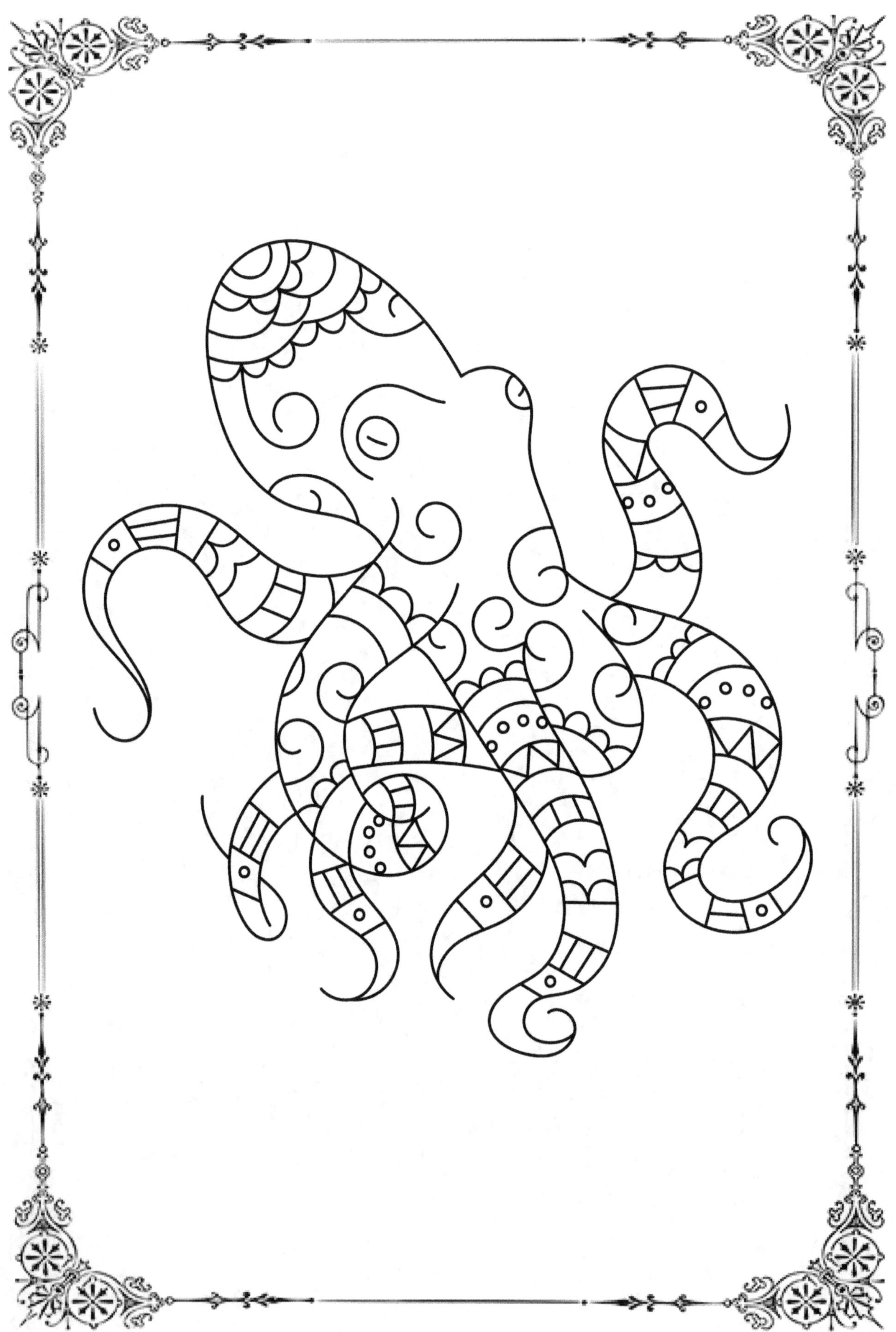

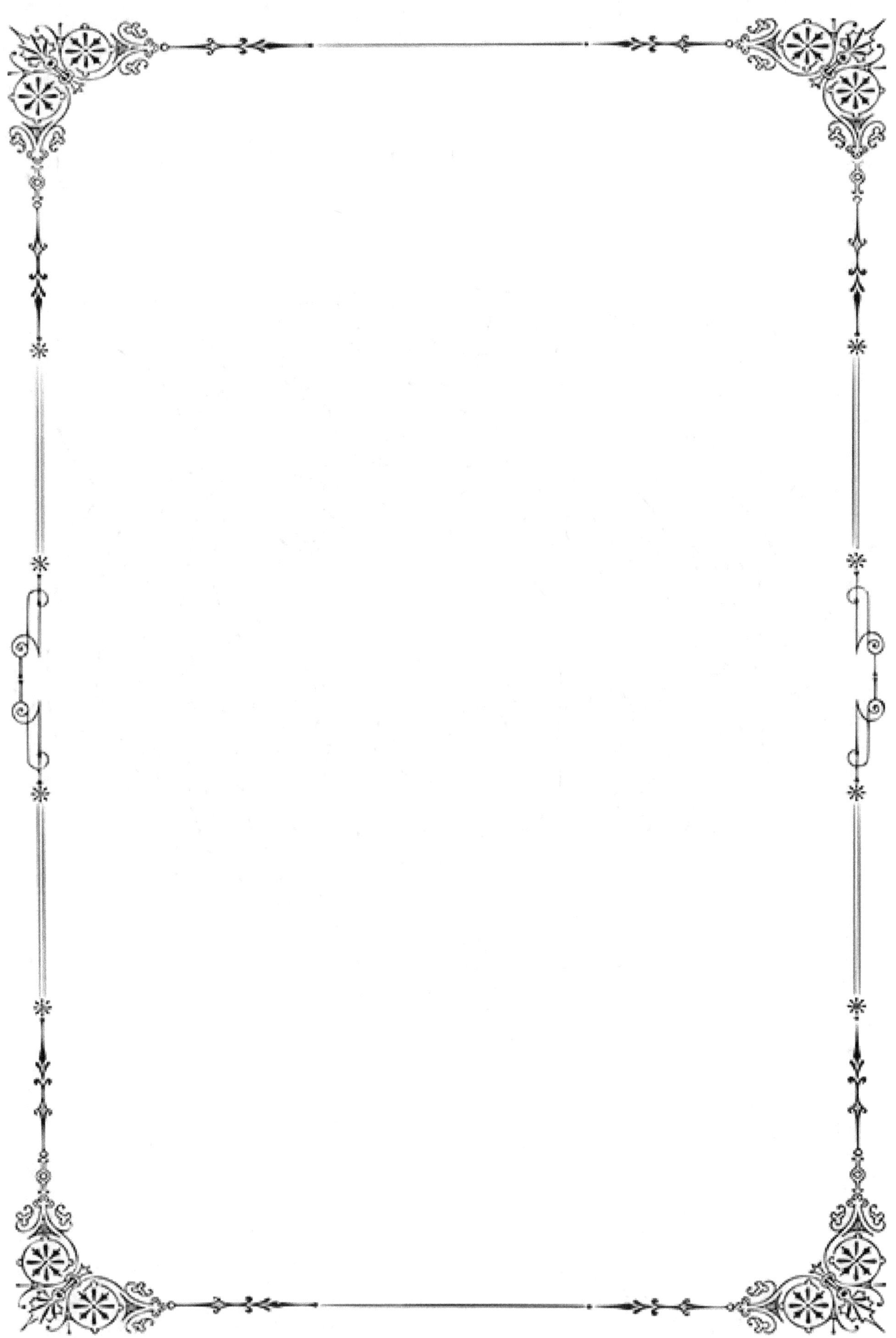

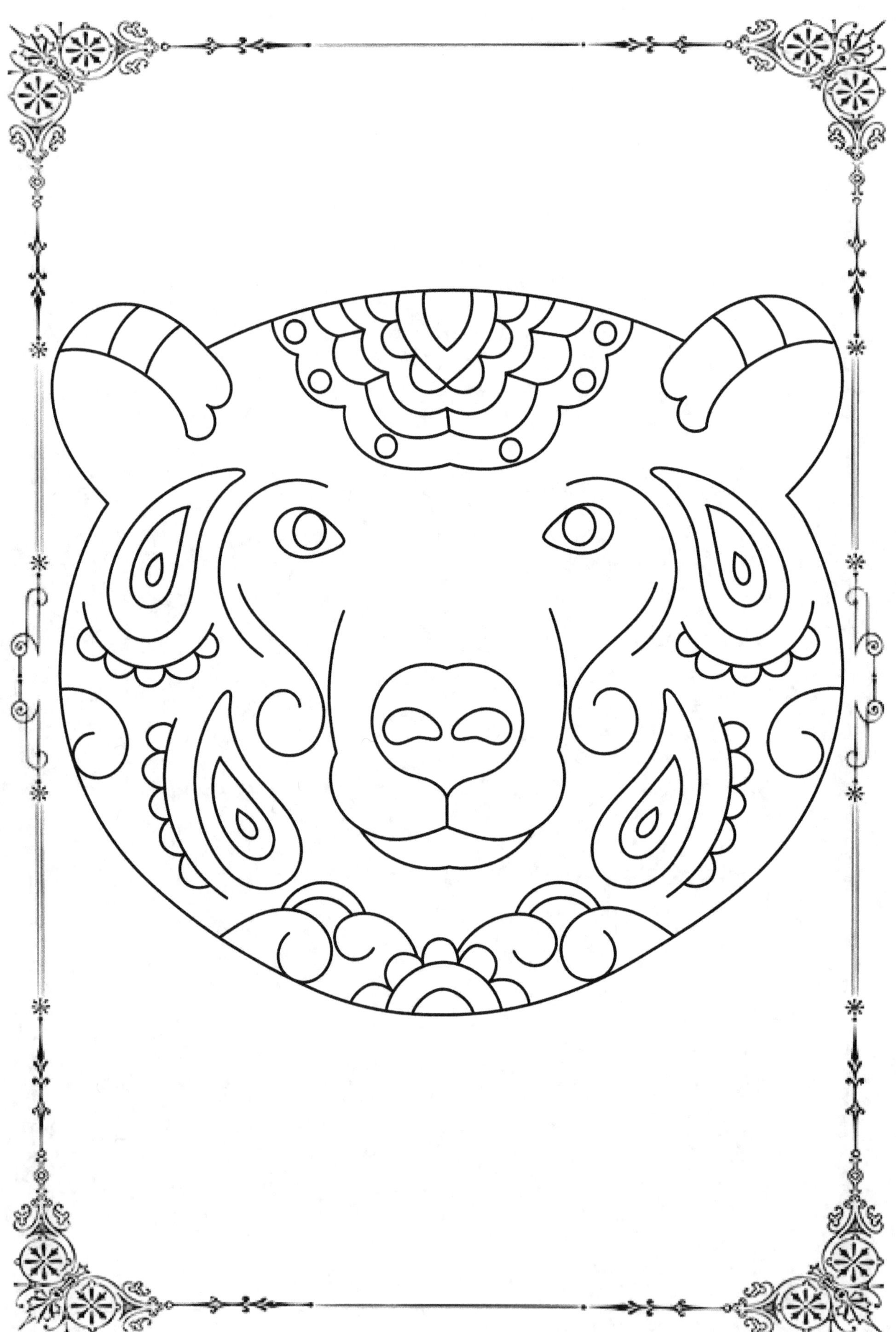

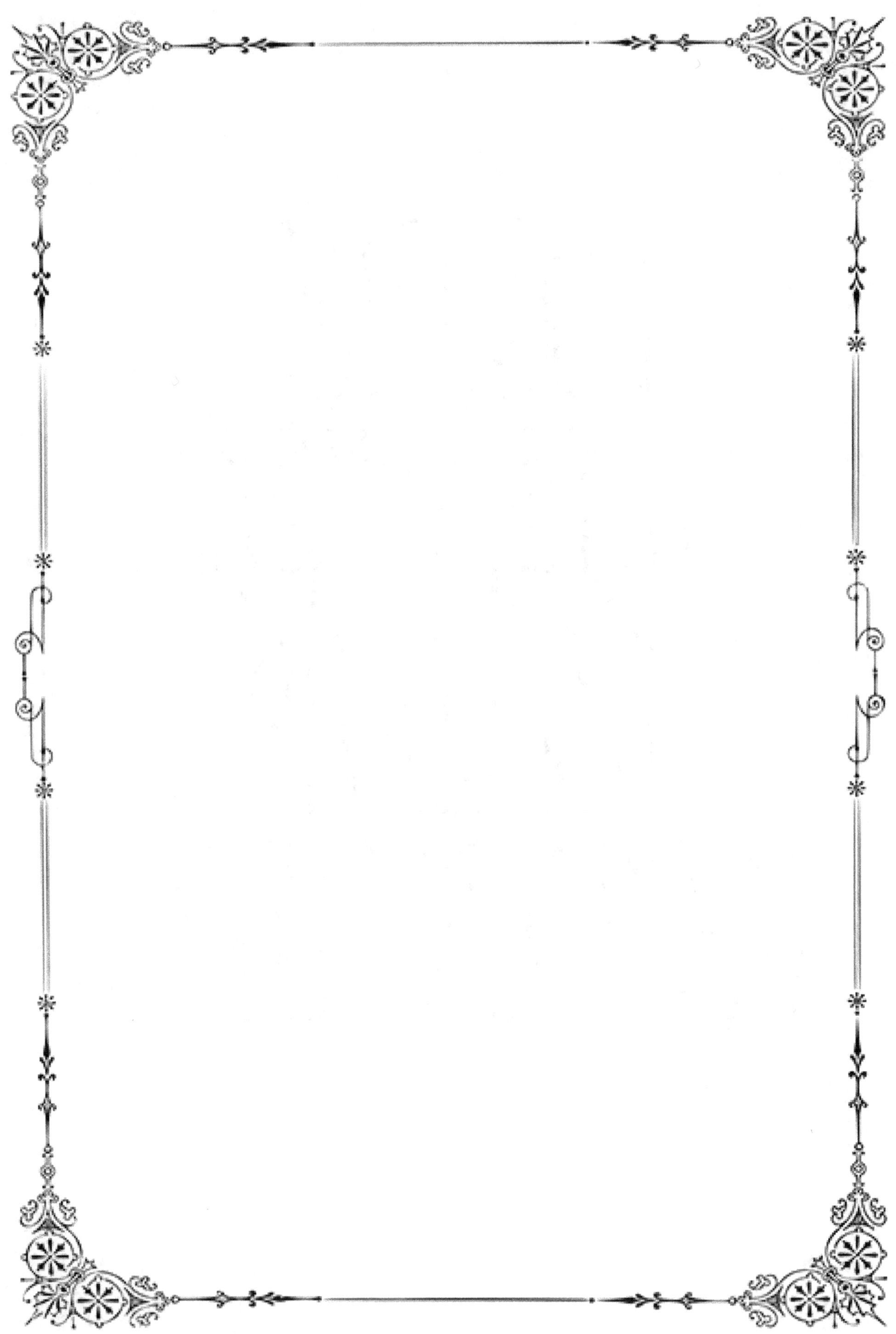

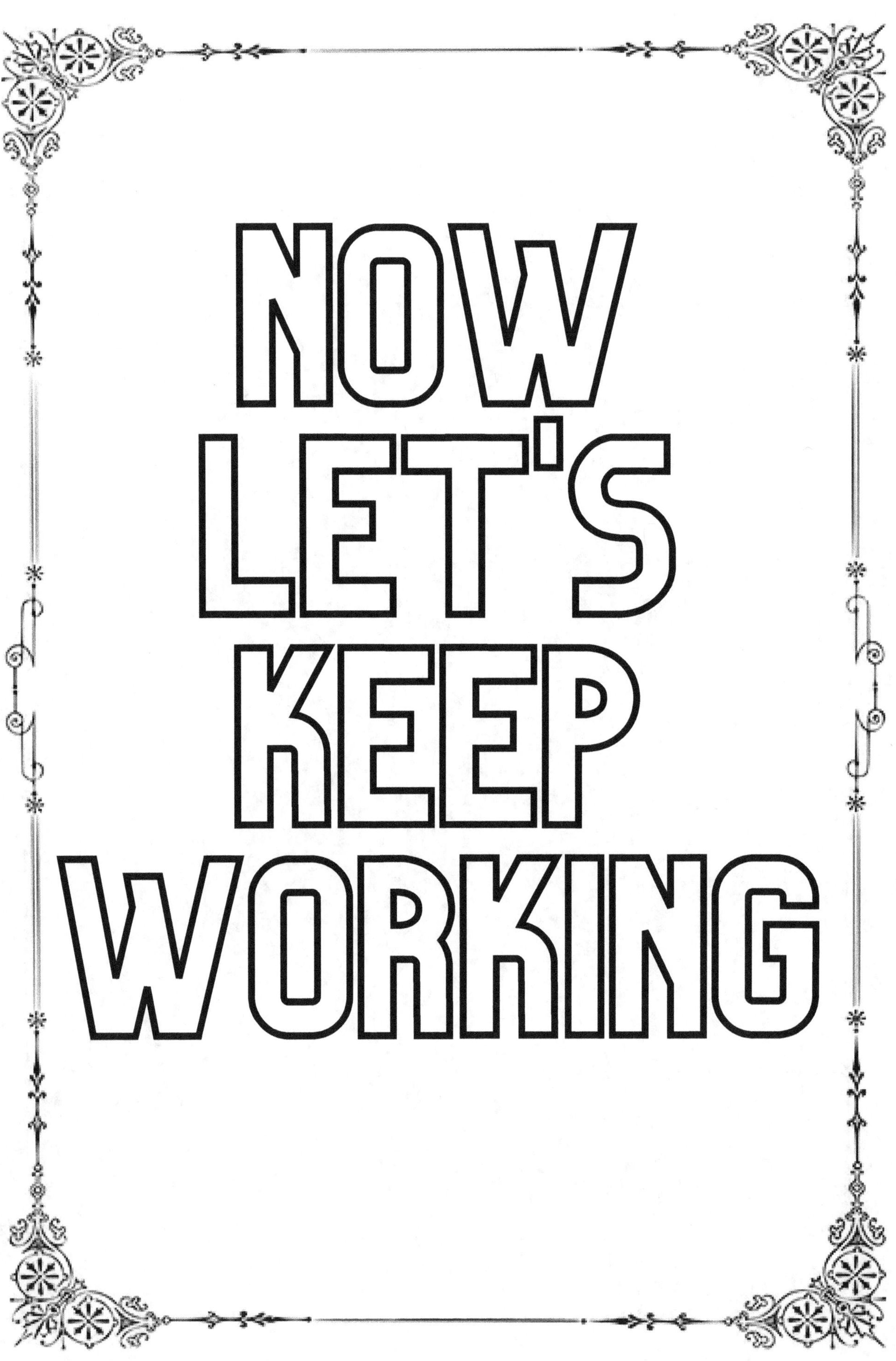

NOW
LET'S
KEEP
WORKING

Gorilla

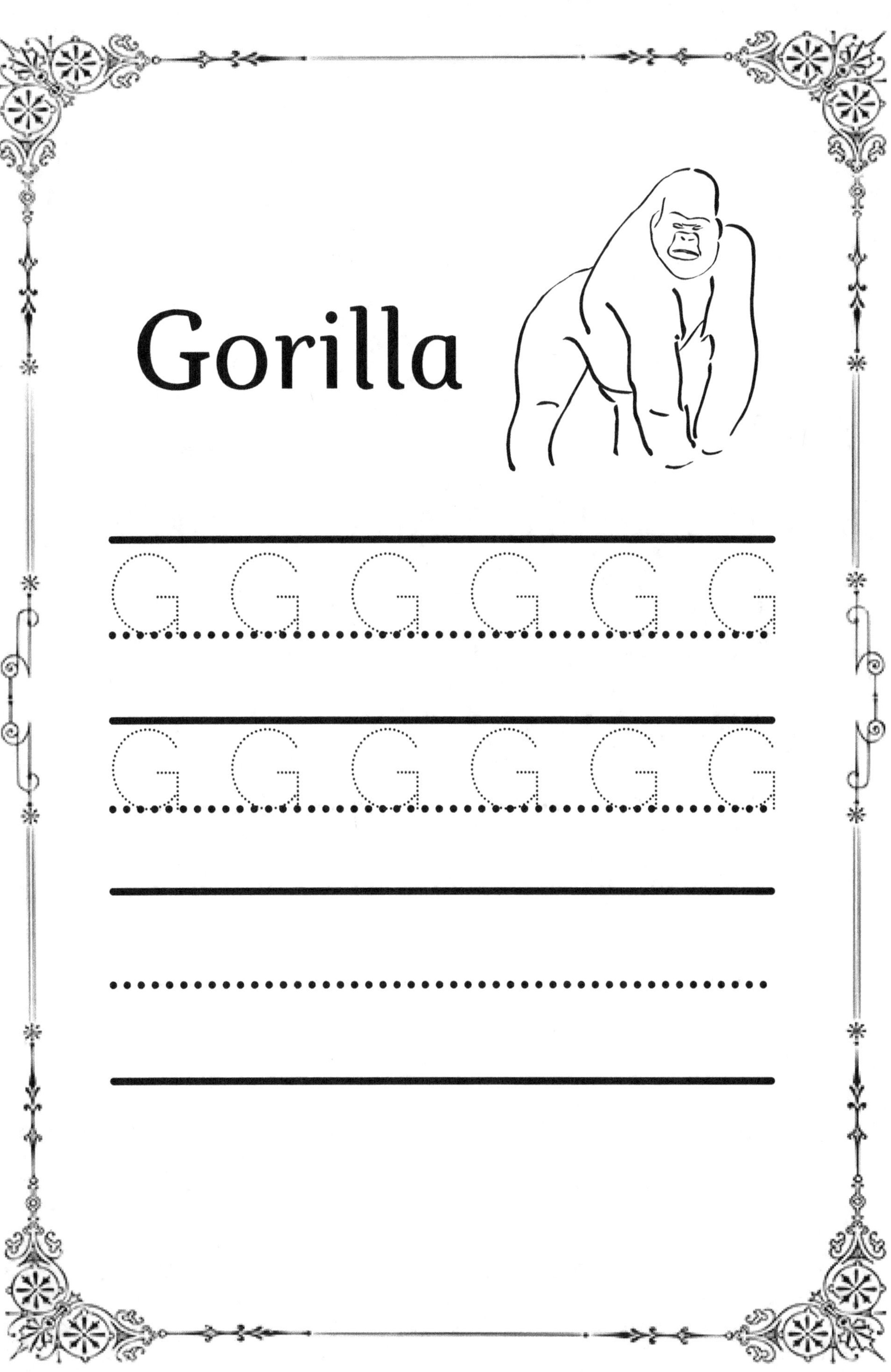

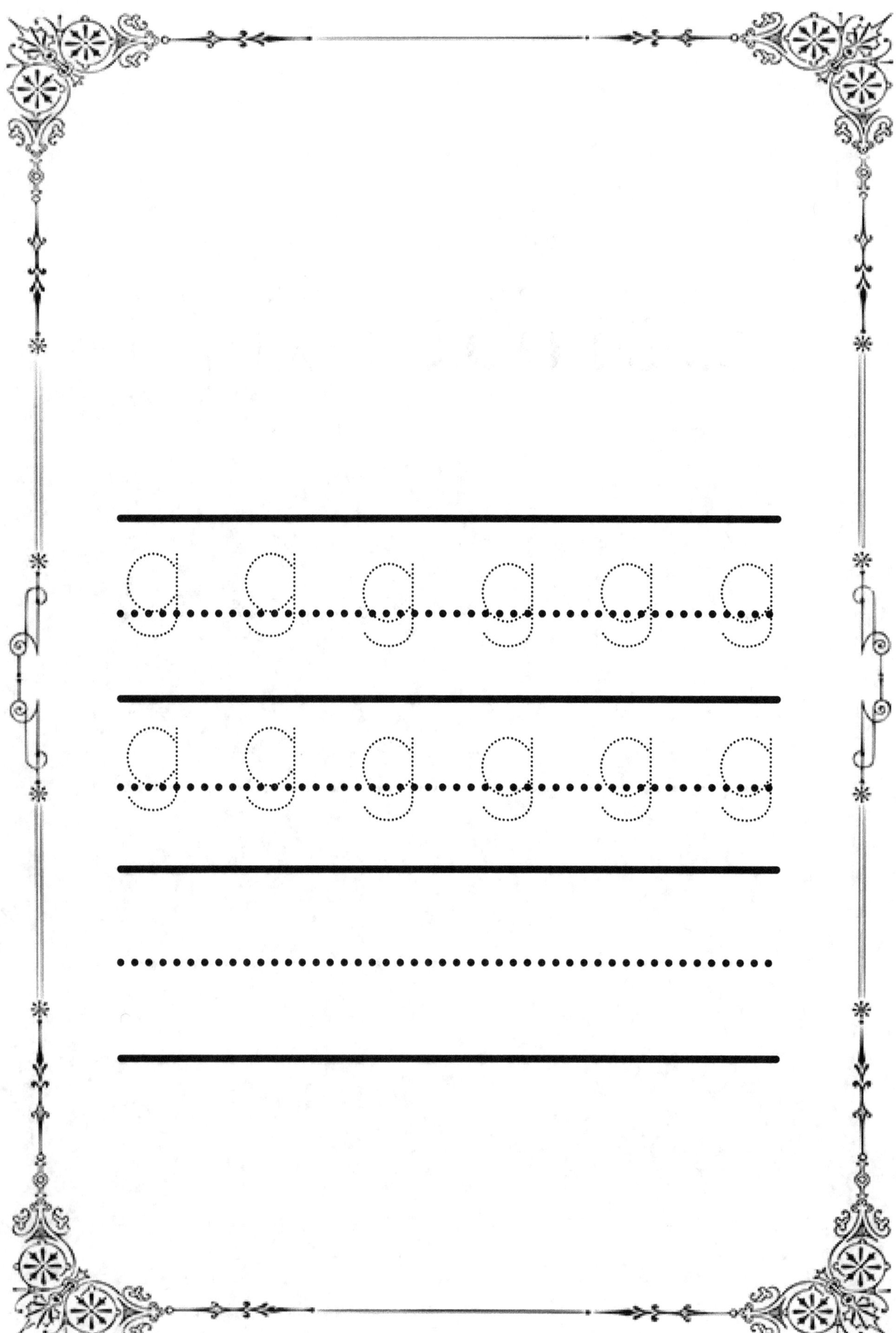

Horse

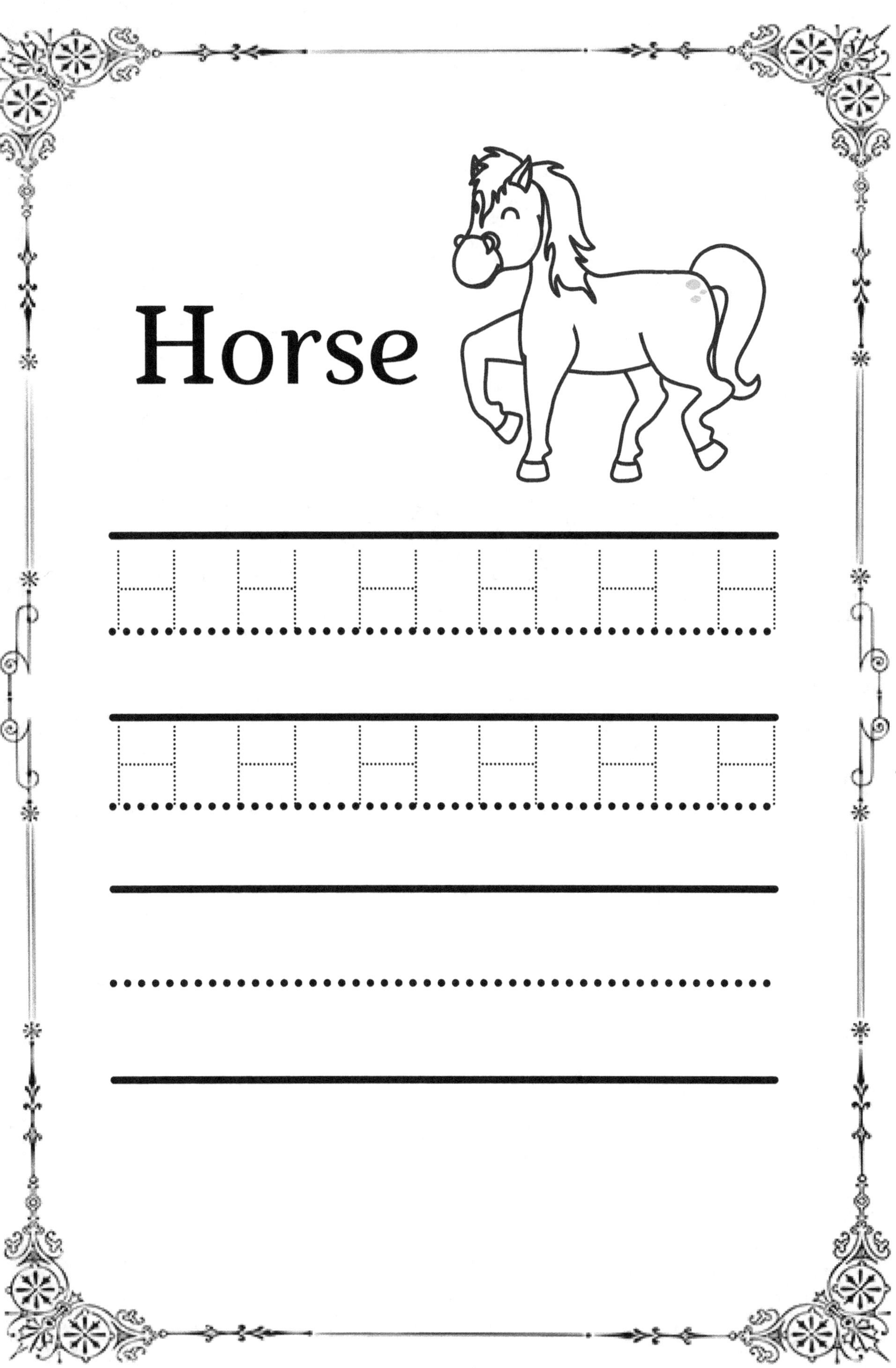

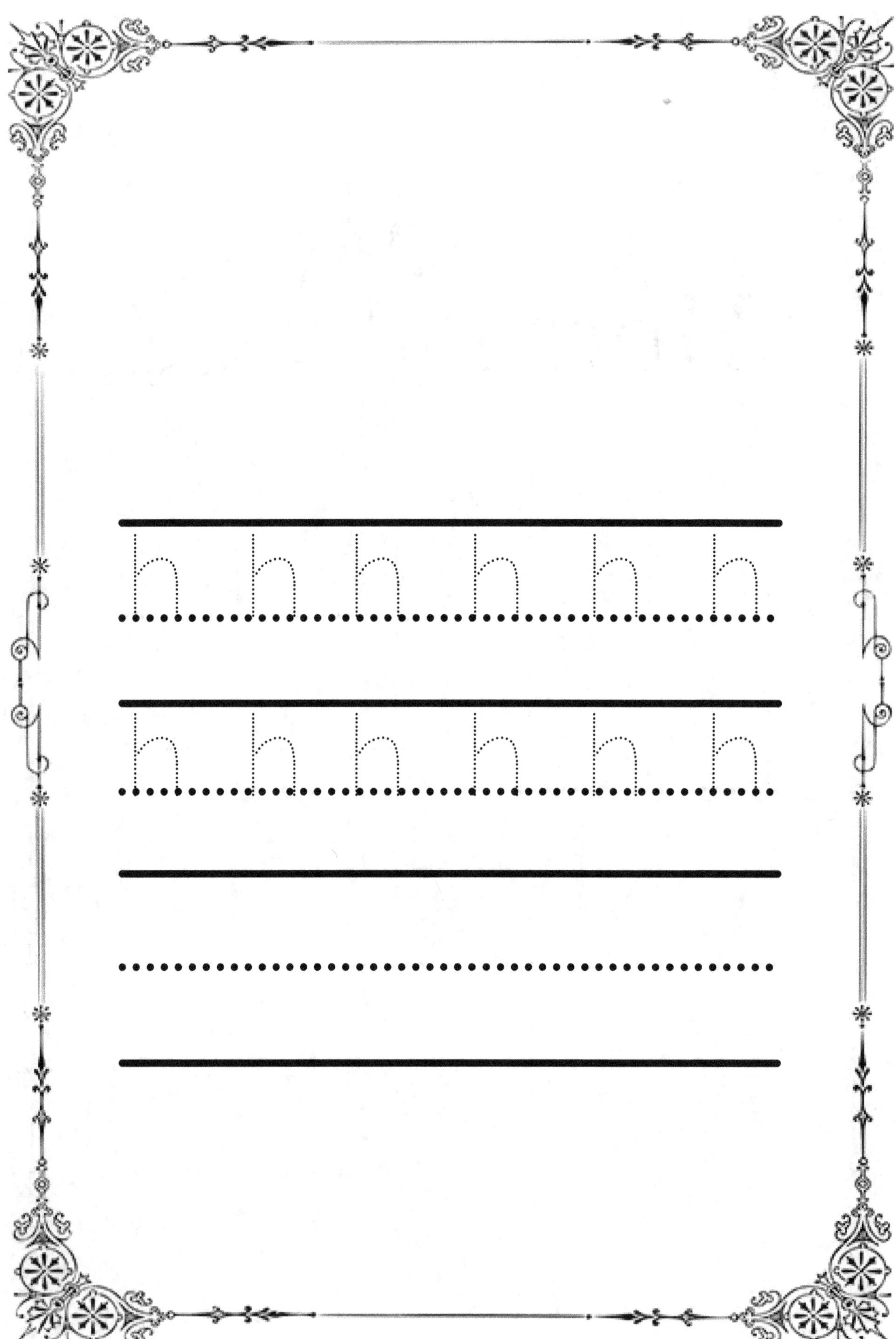

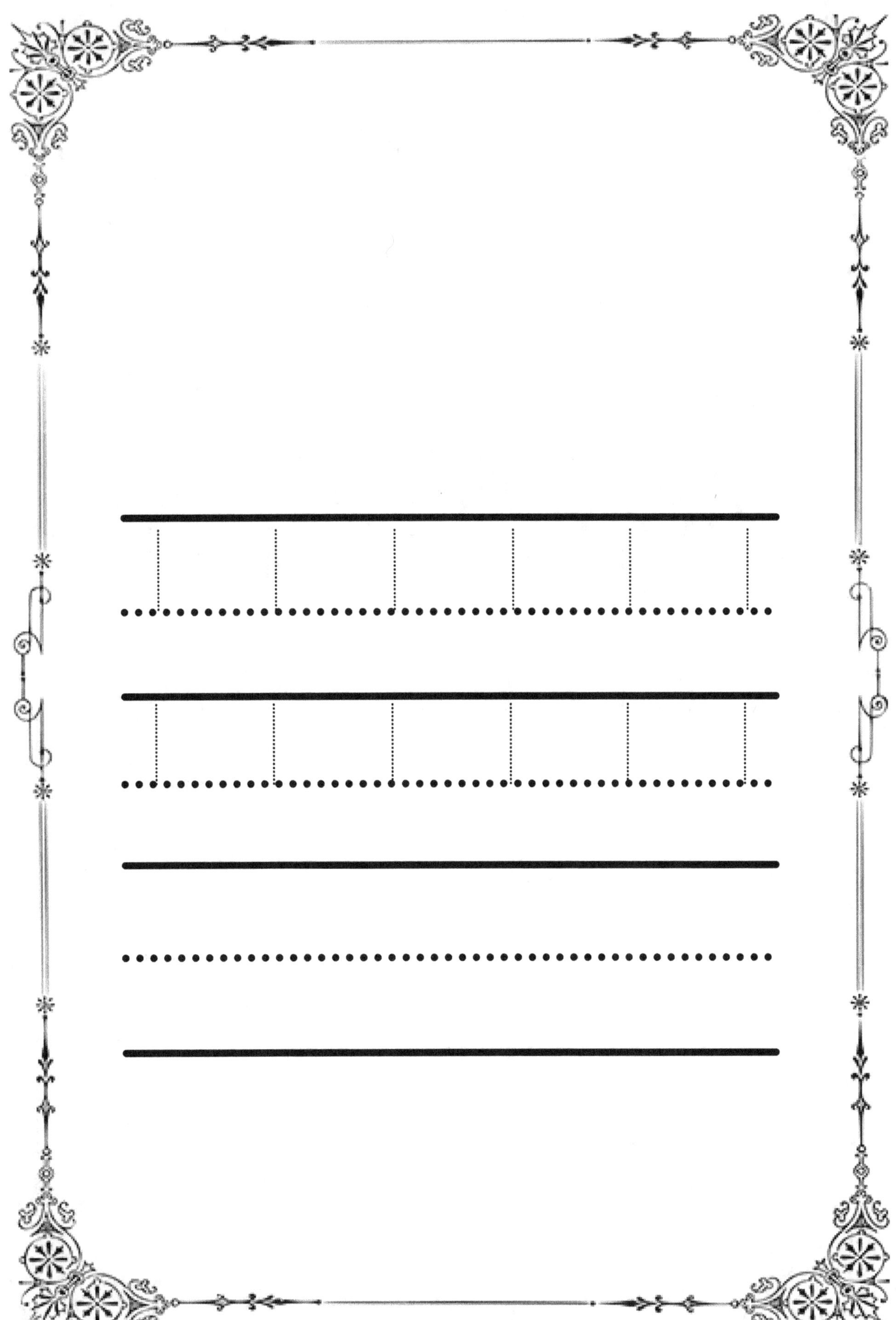

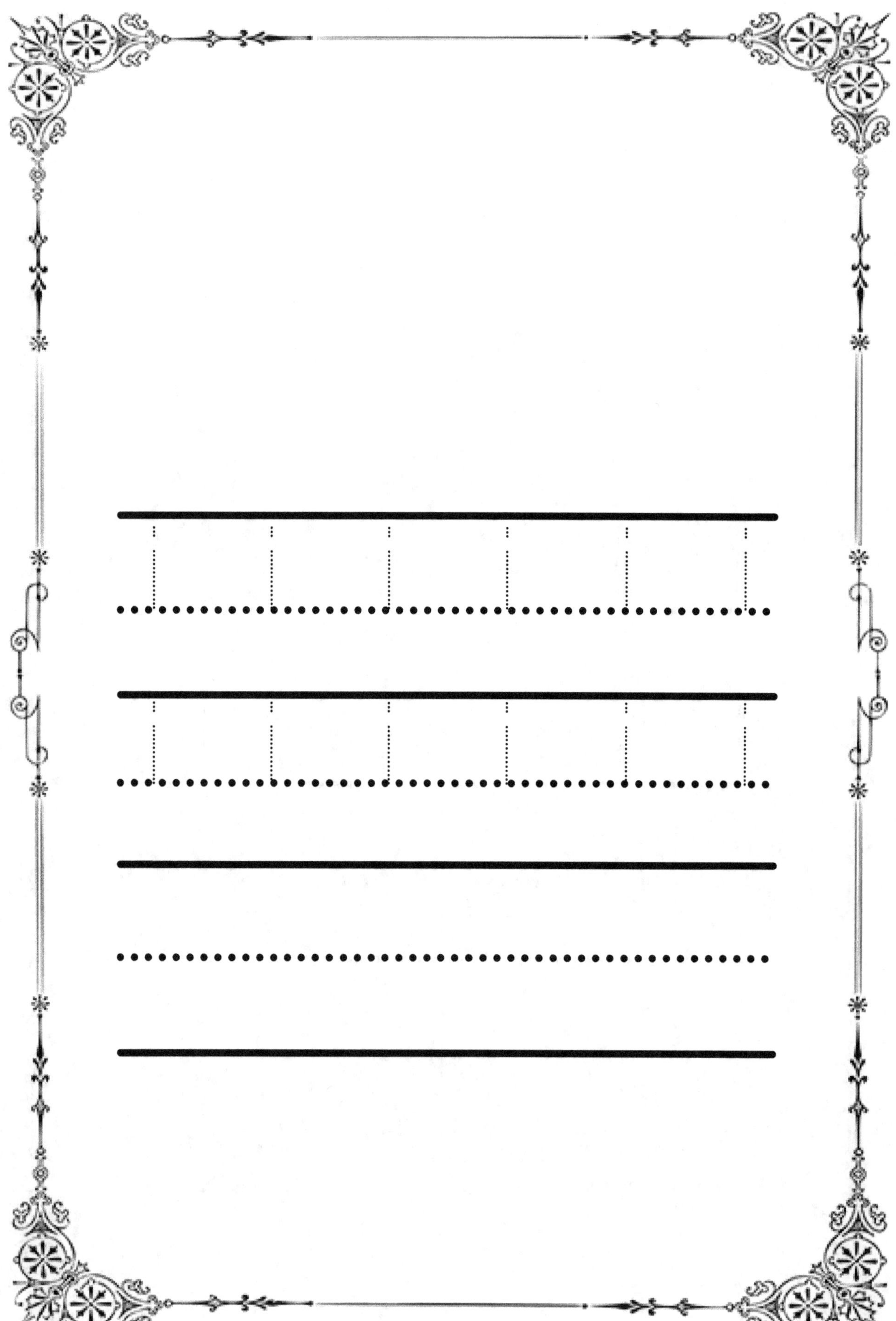

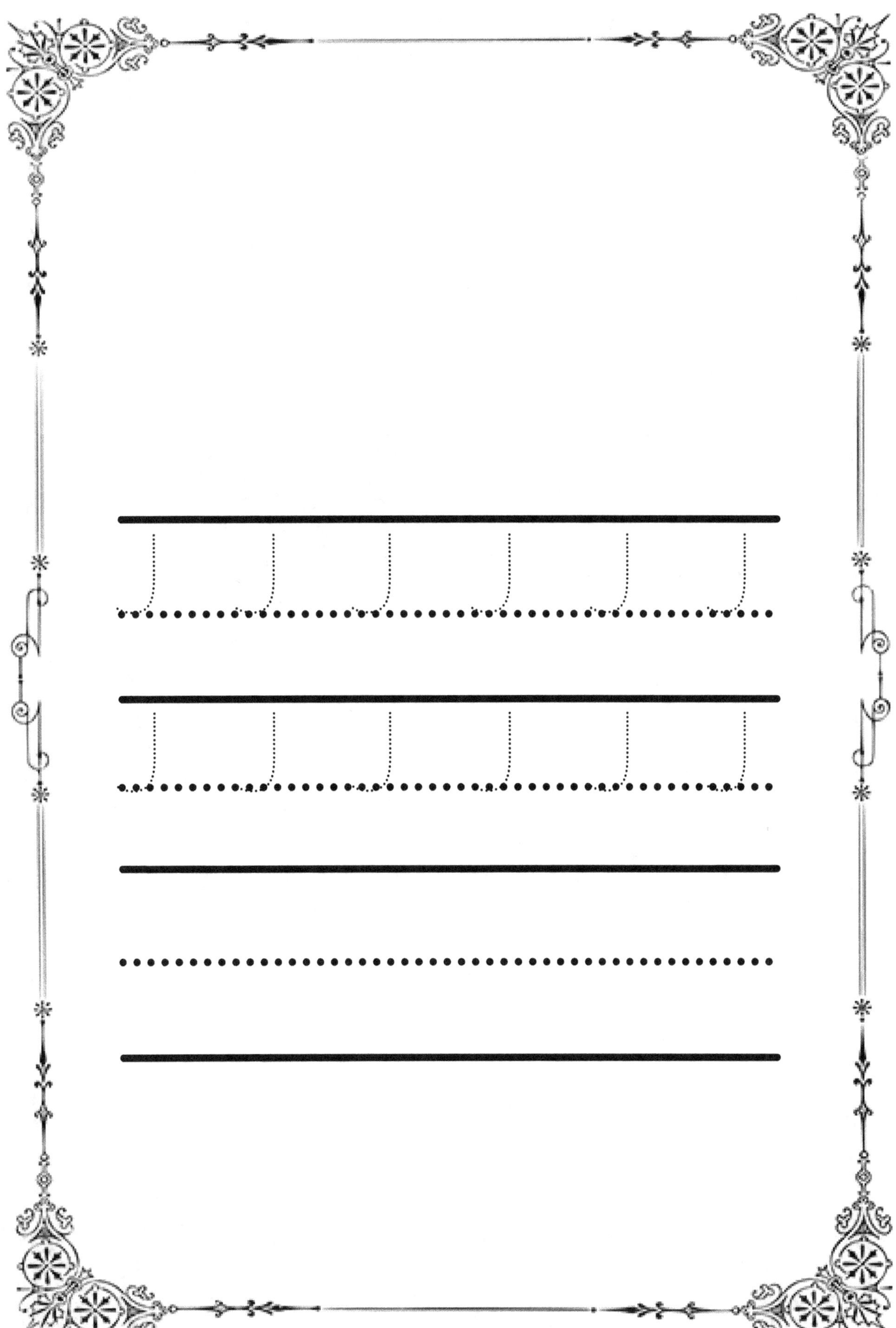

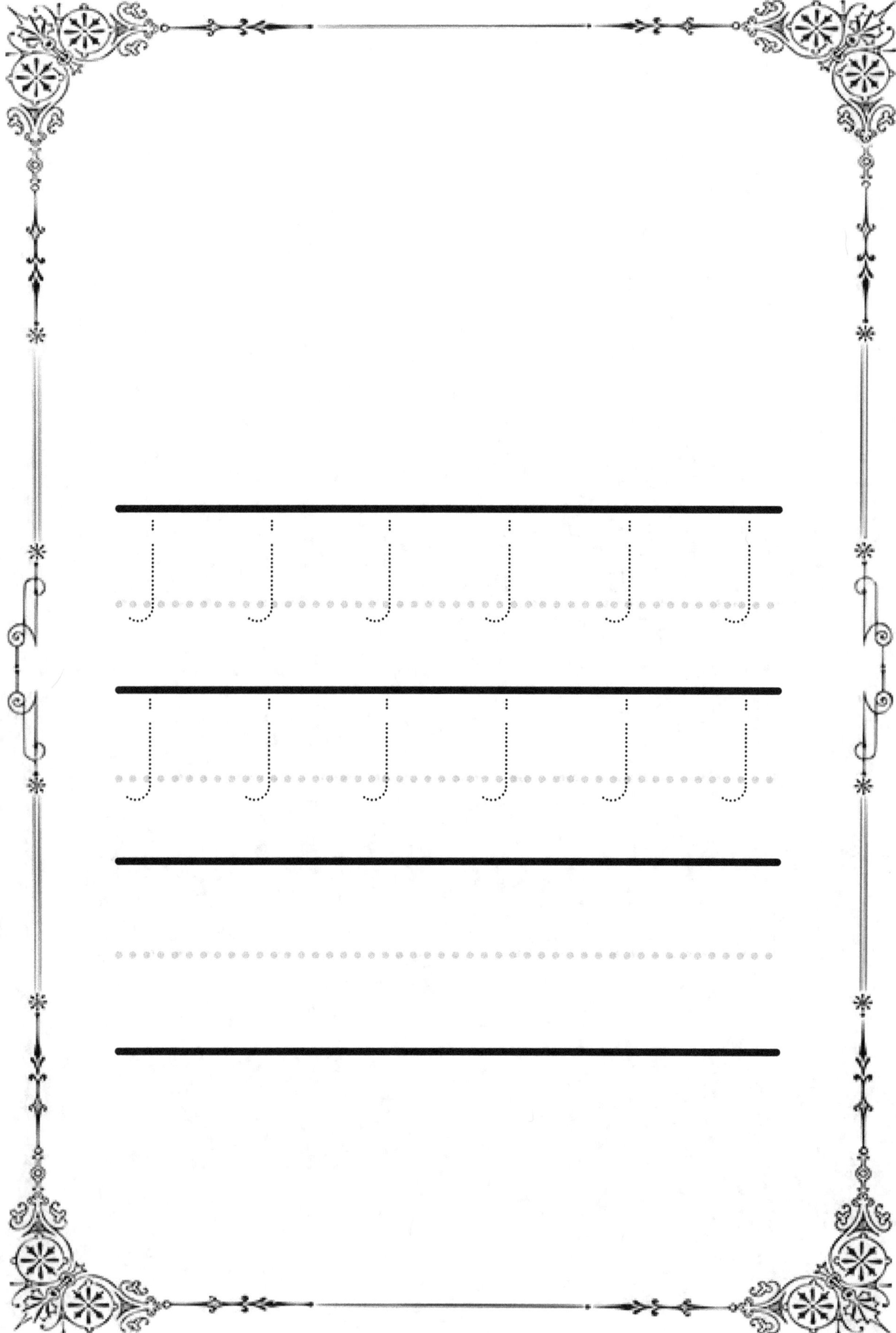

Kangaroo

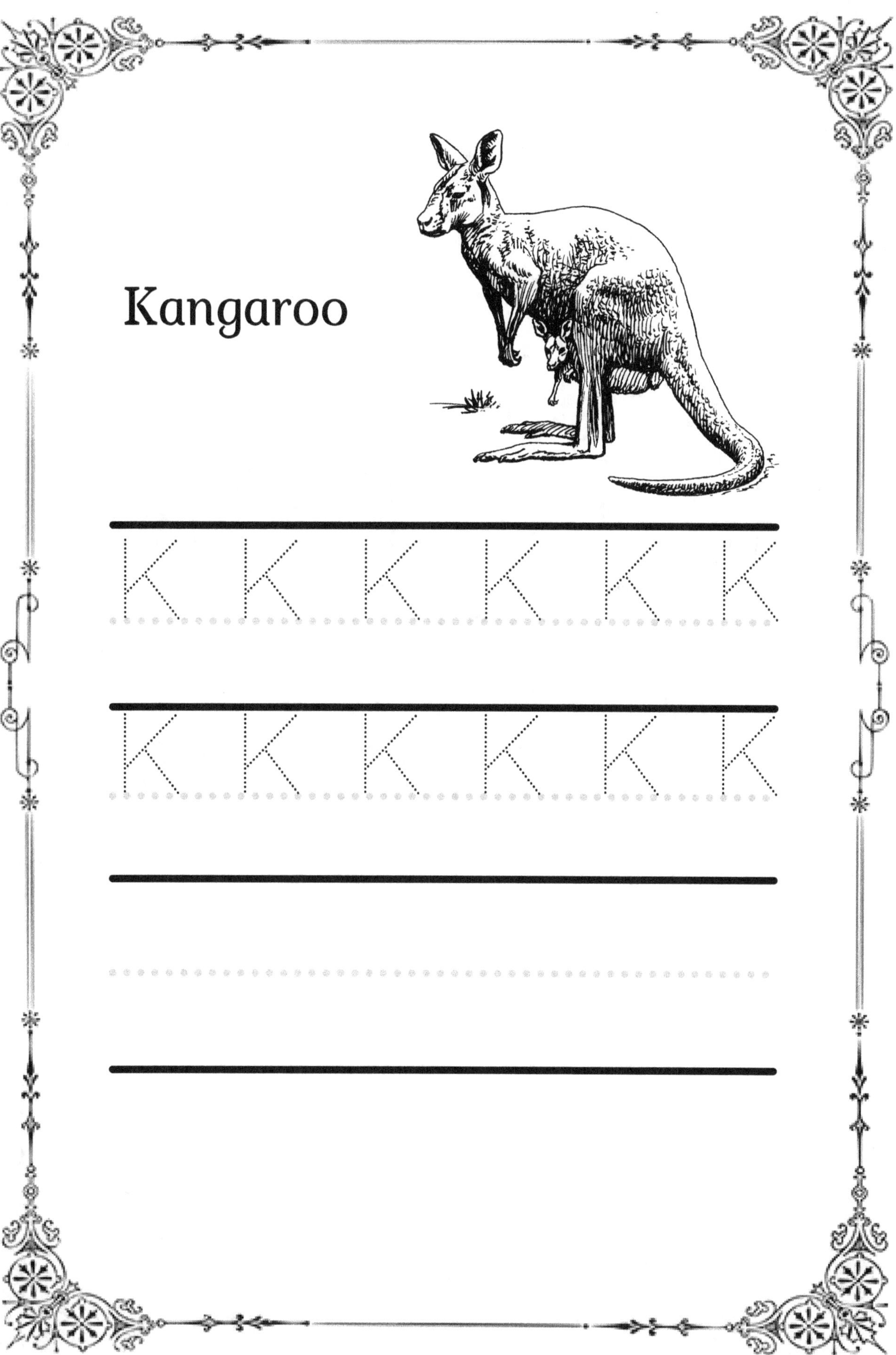

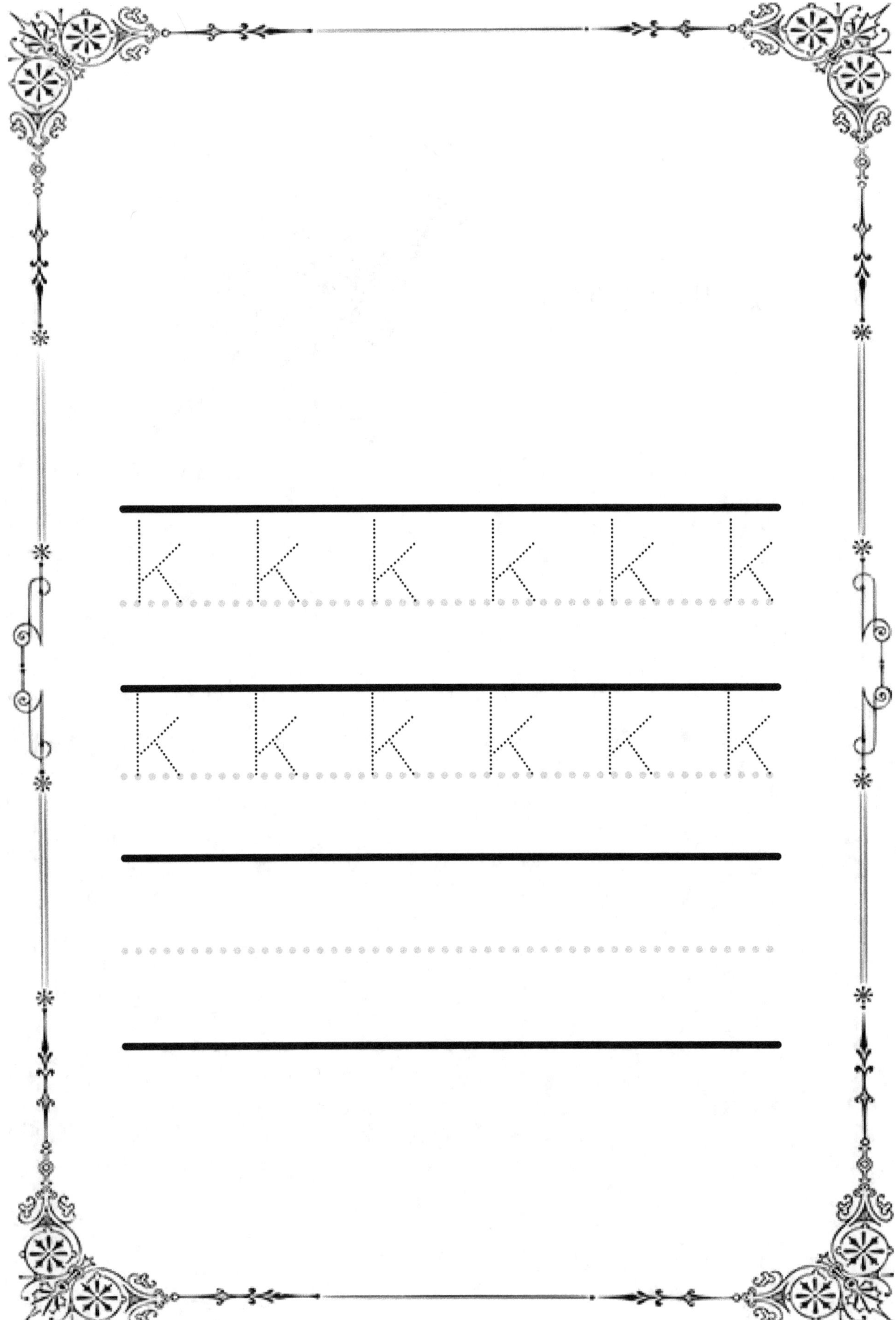

Lion

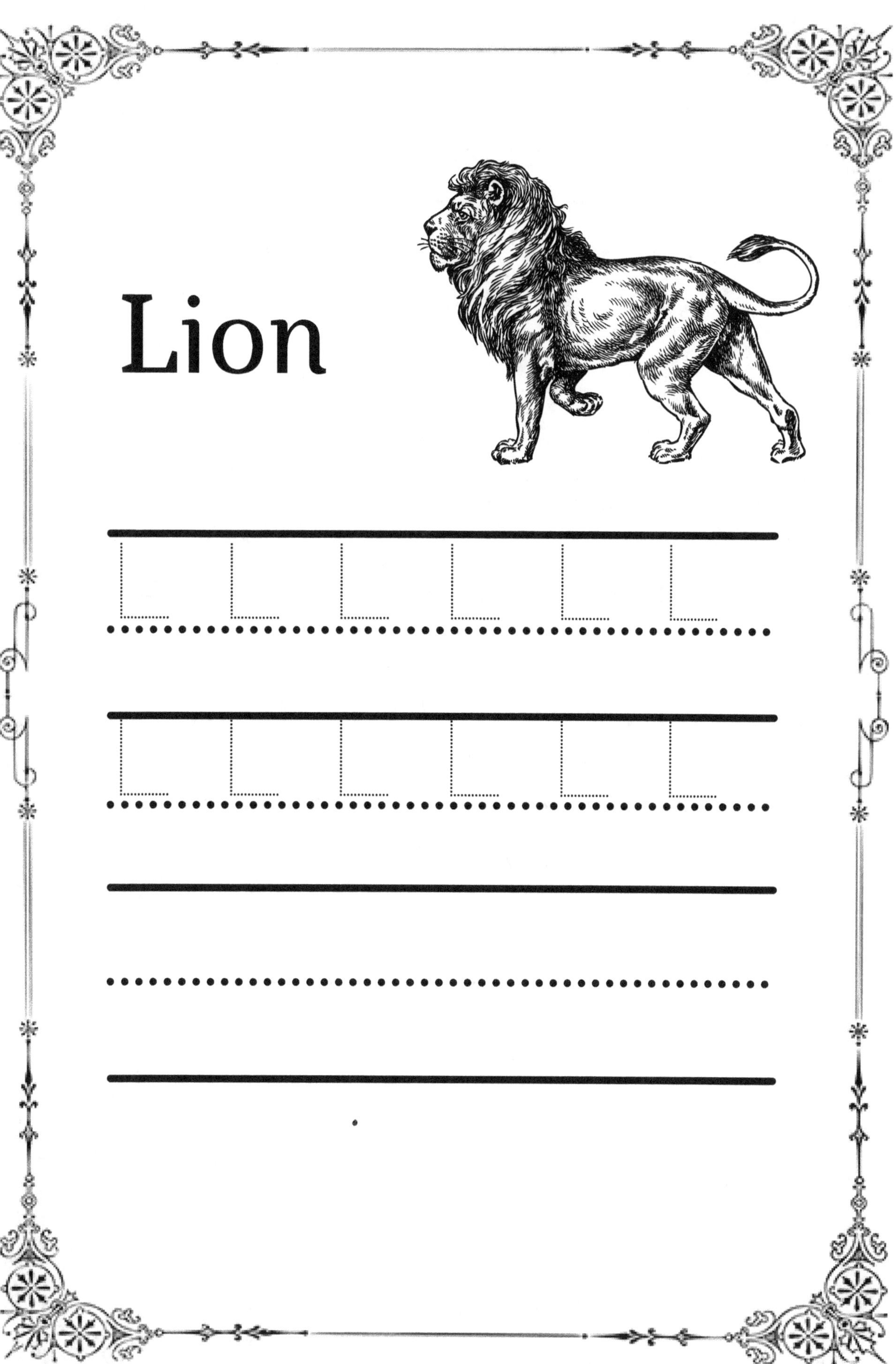

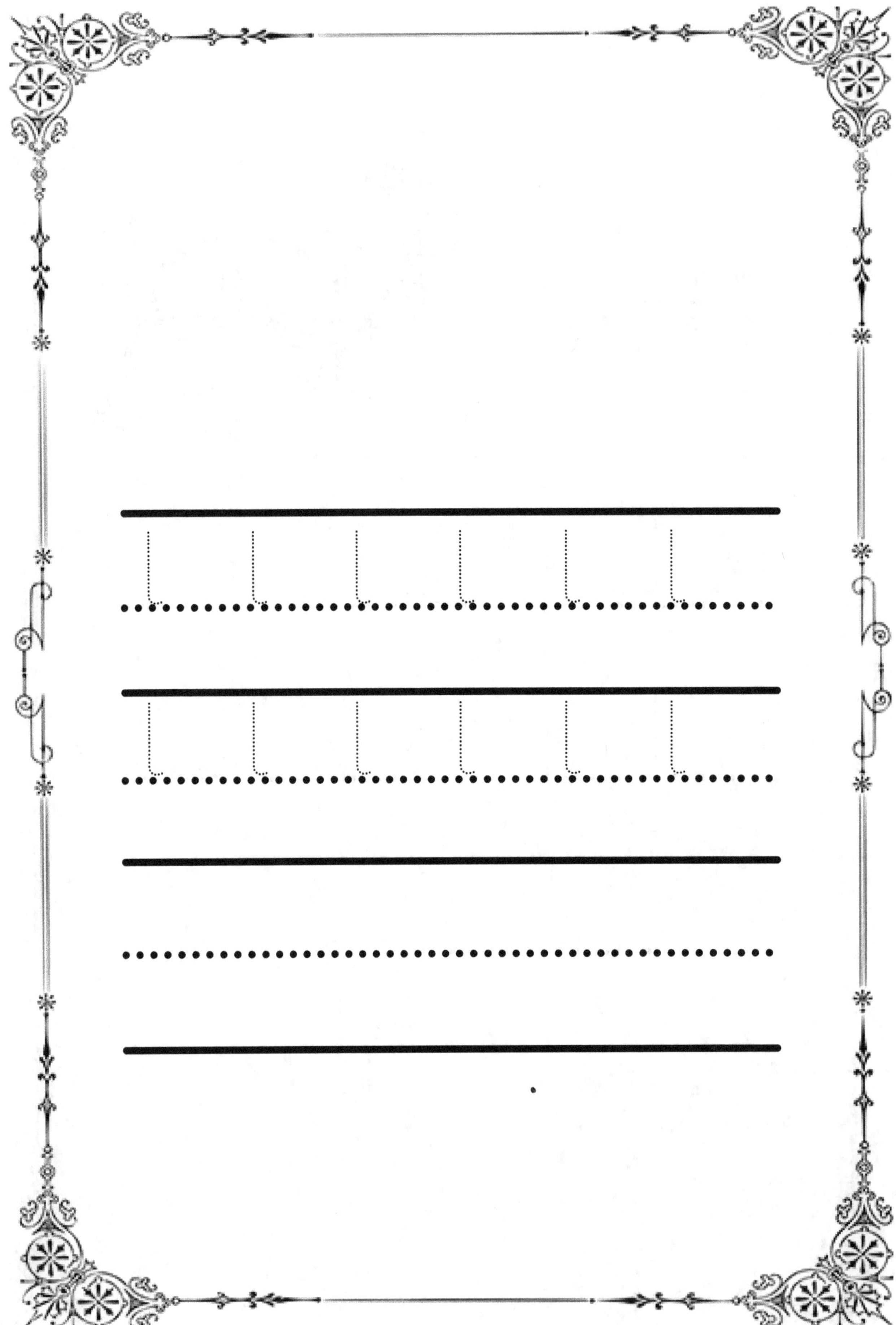

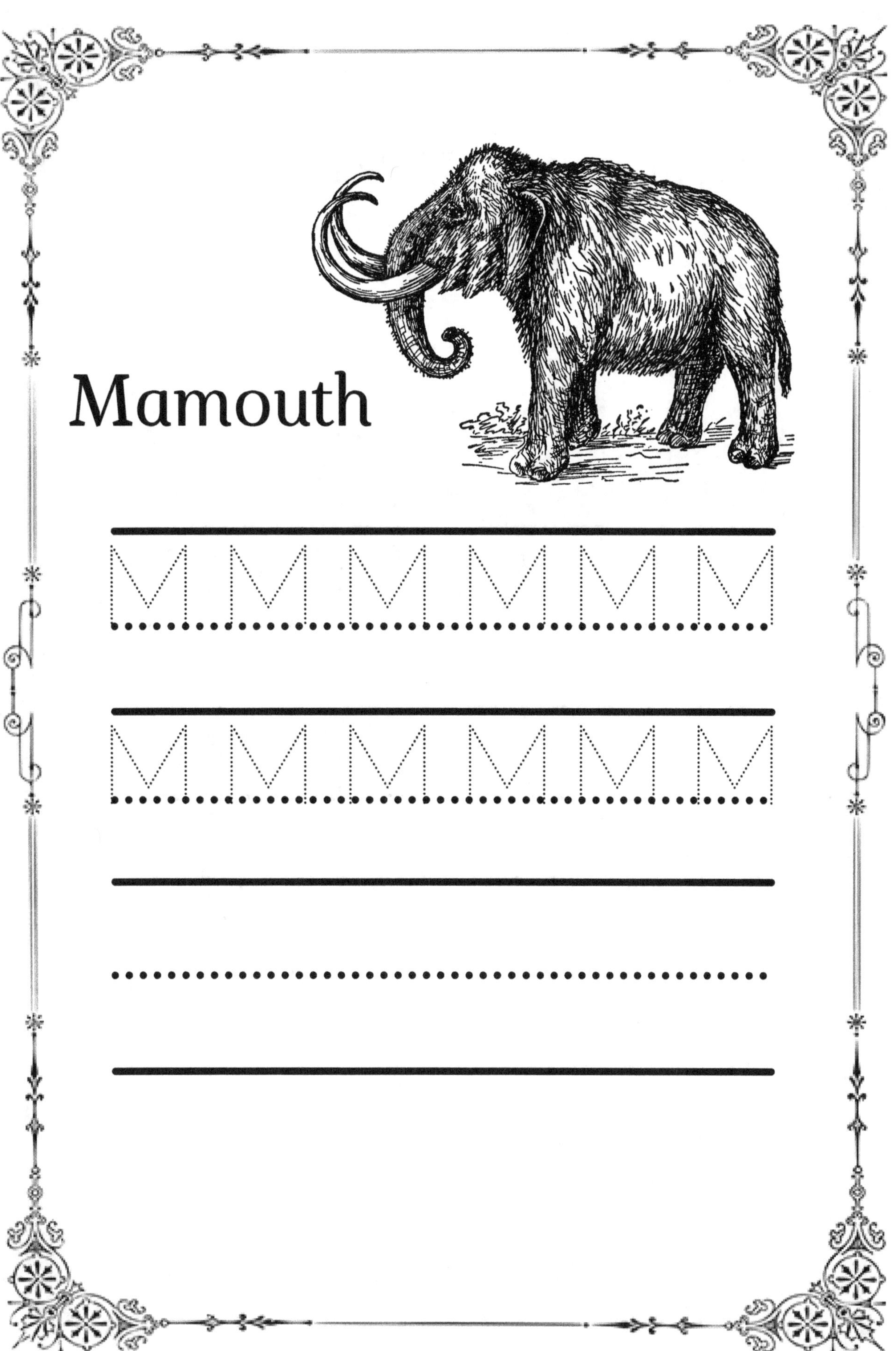

Mamouth

M.M.M.M.M.M.M.M

M.M.M.M.M.M.M.M

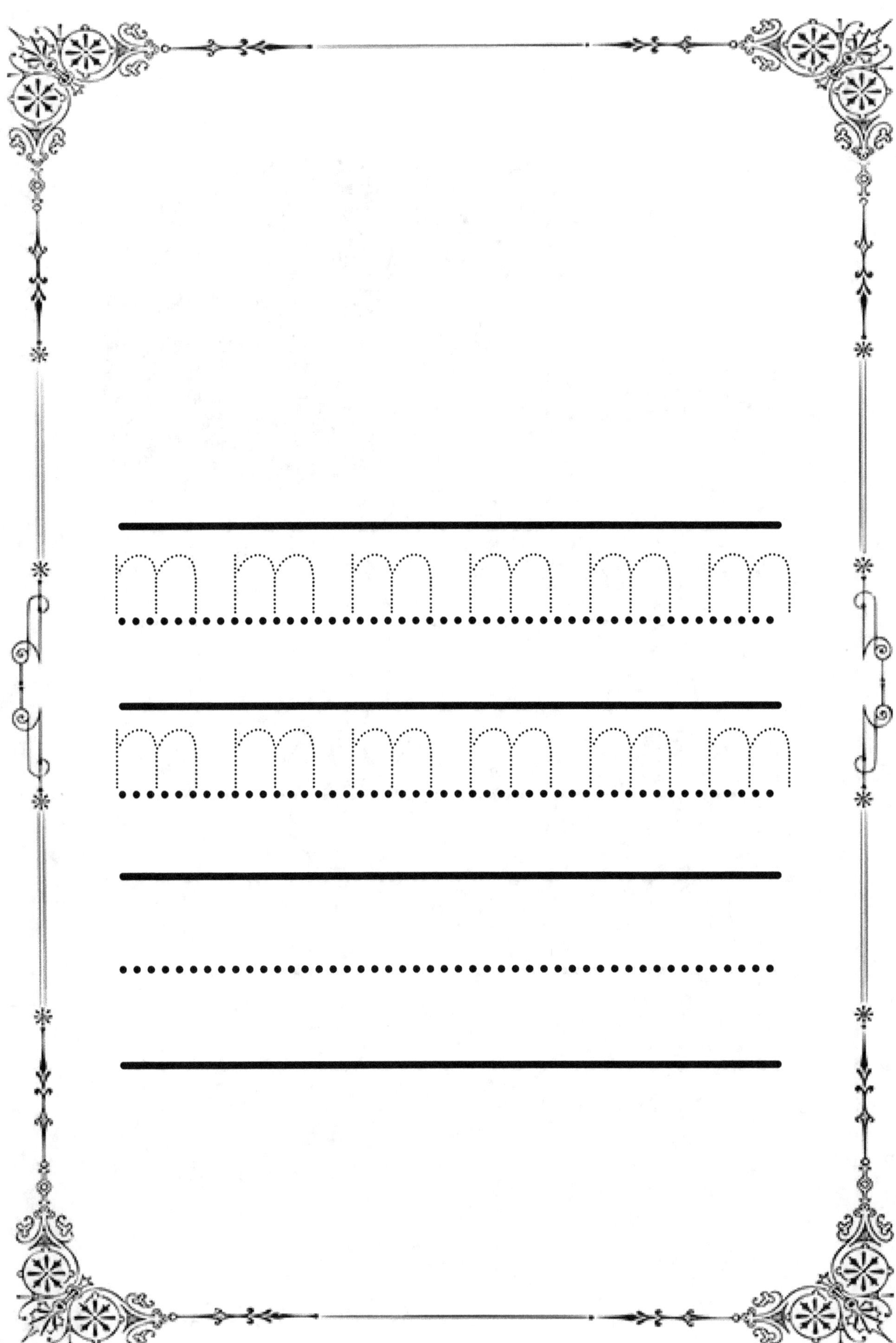

HOW MUCH DOES A PIRATE PAY FOR CORN?
A BUCCANEER!

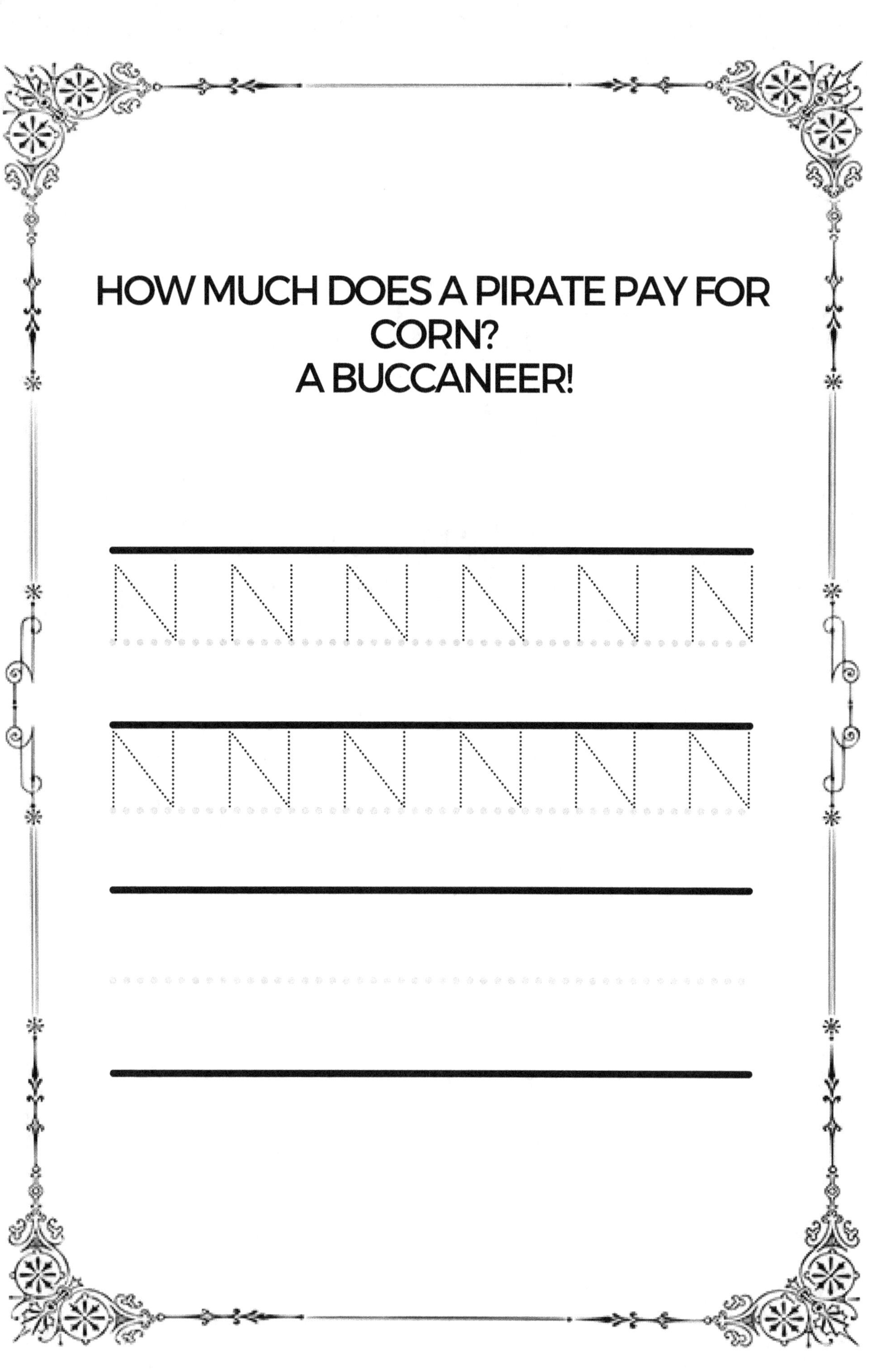

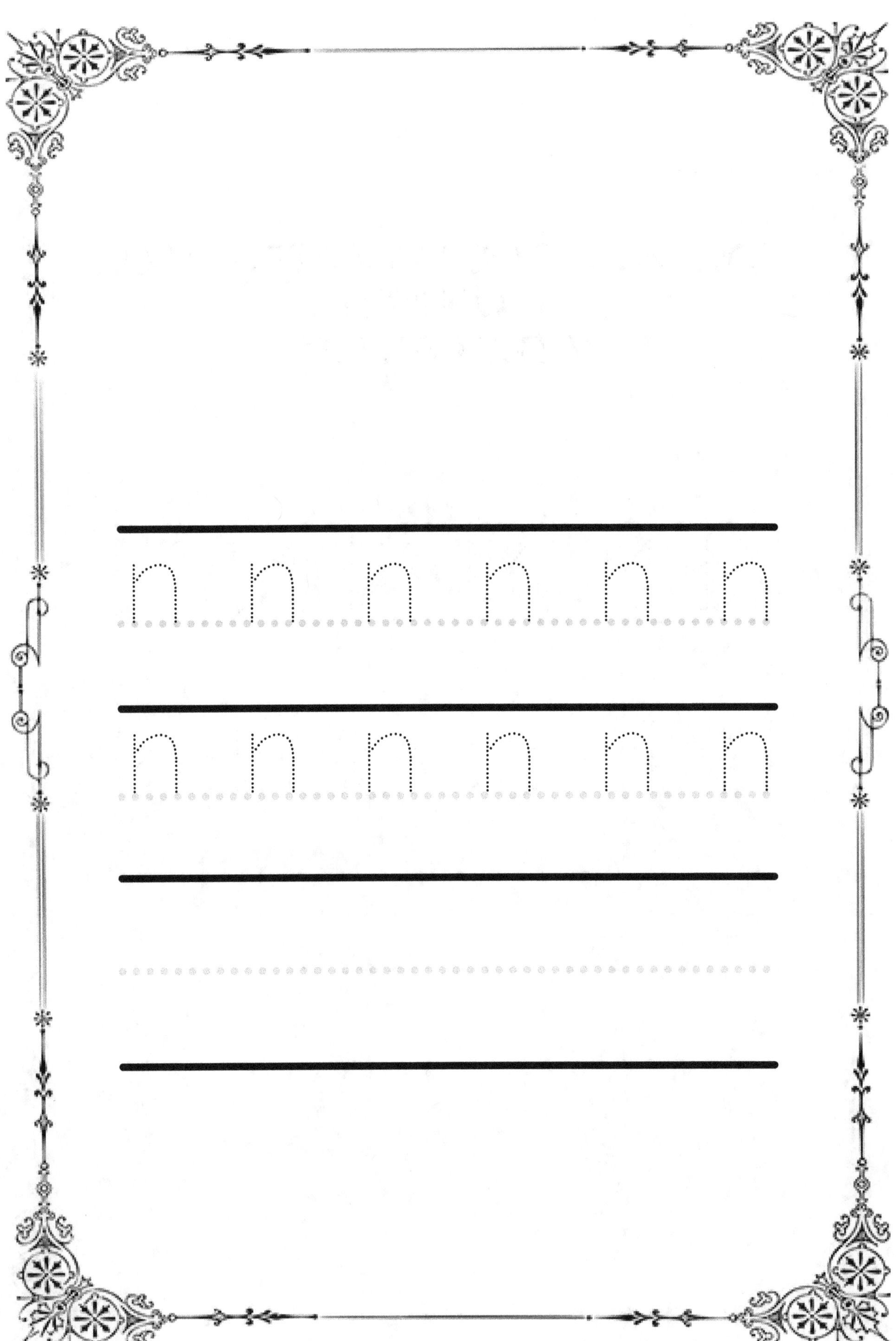

Octupos

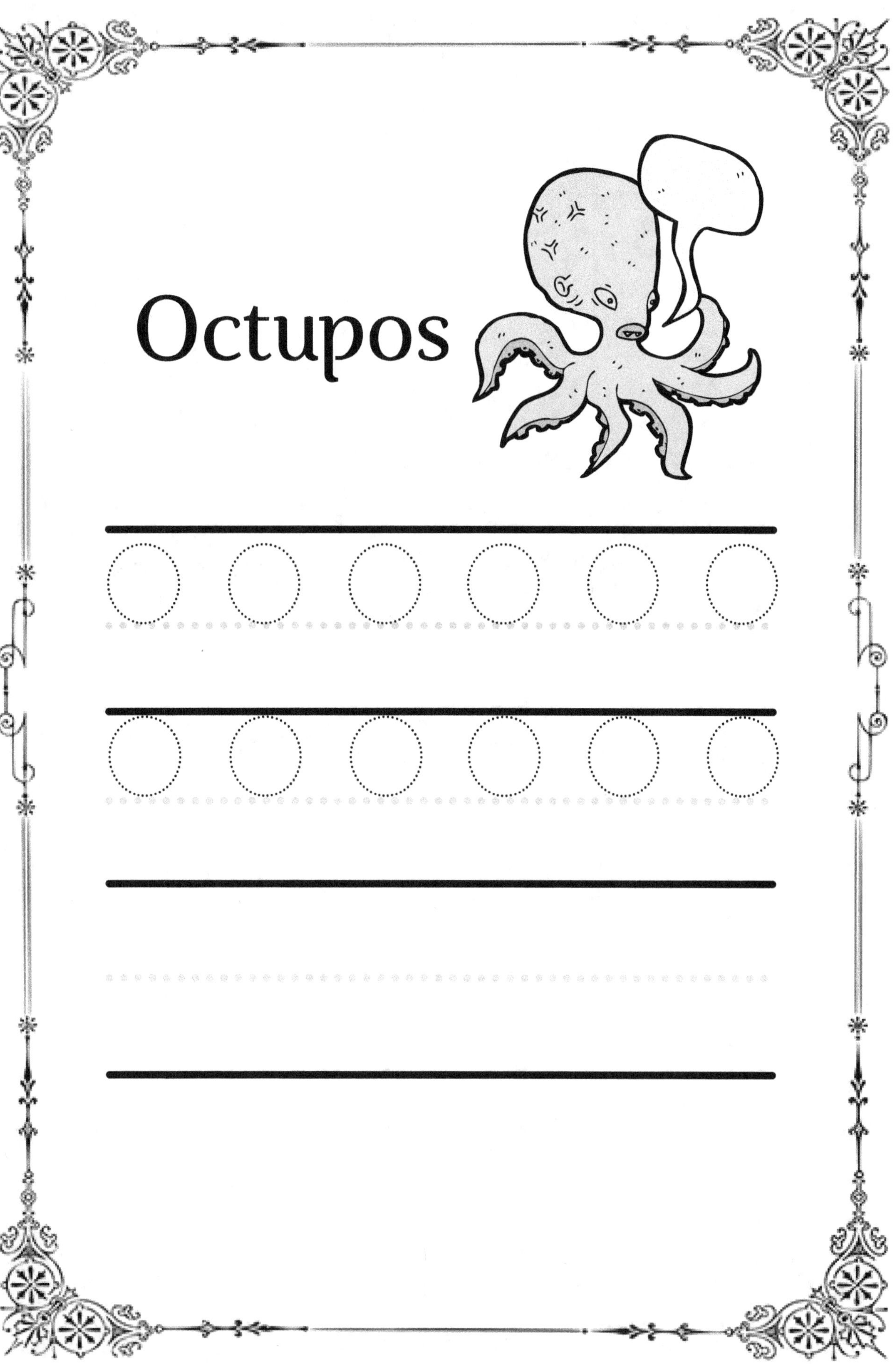

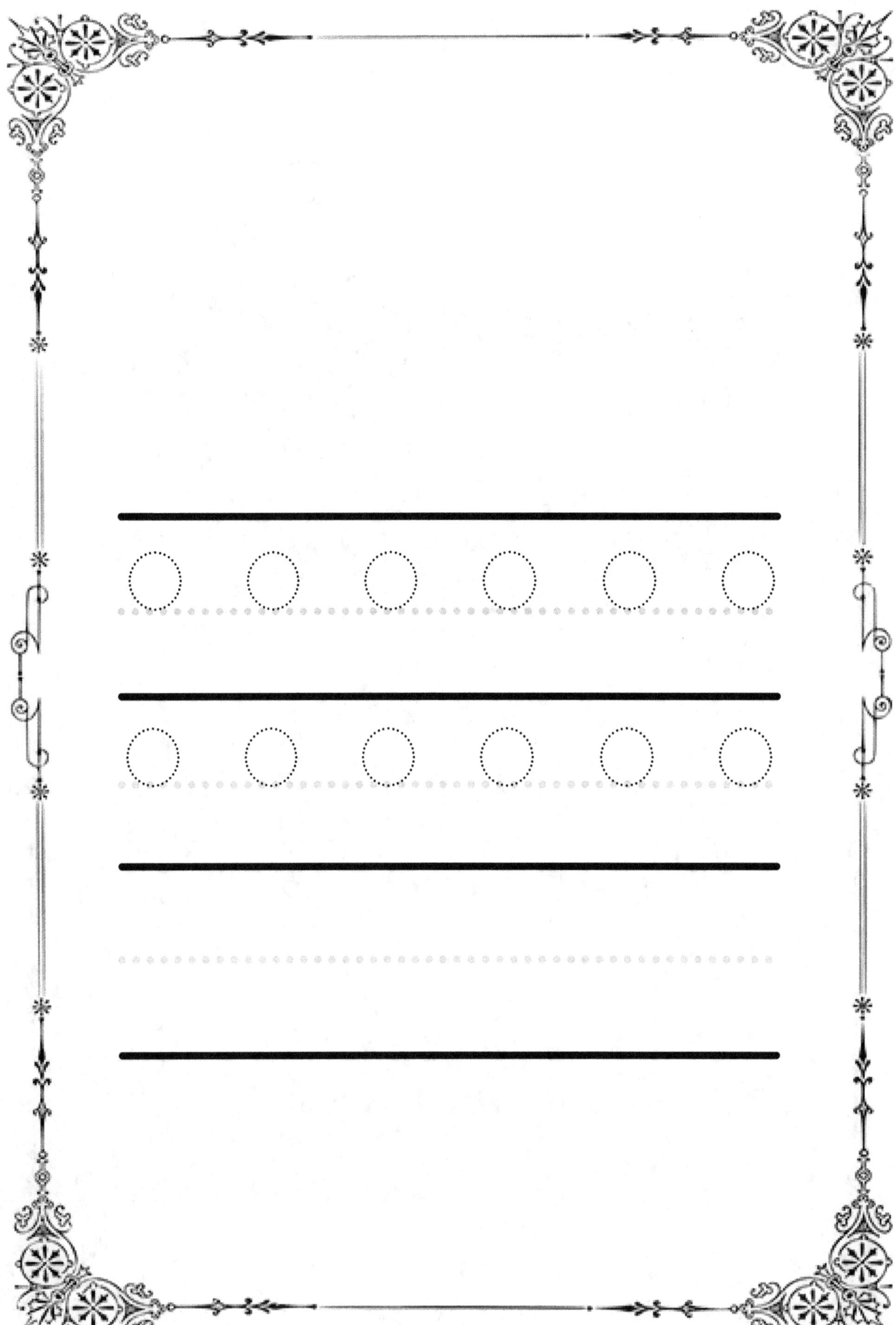

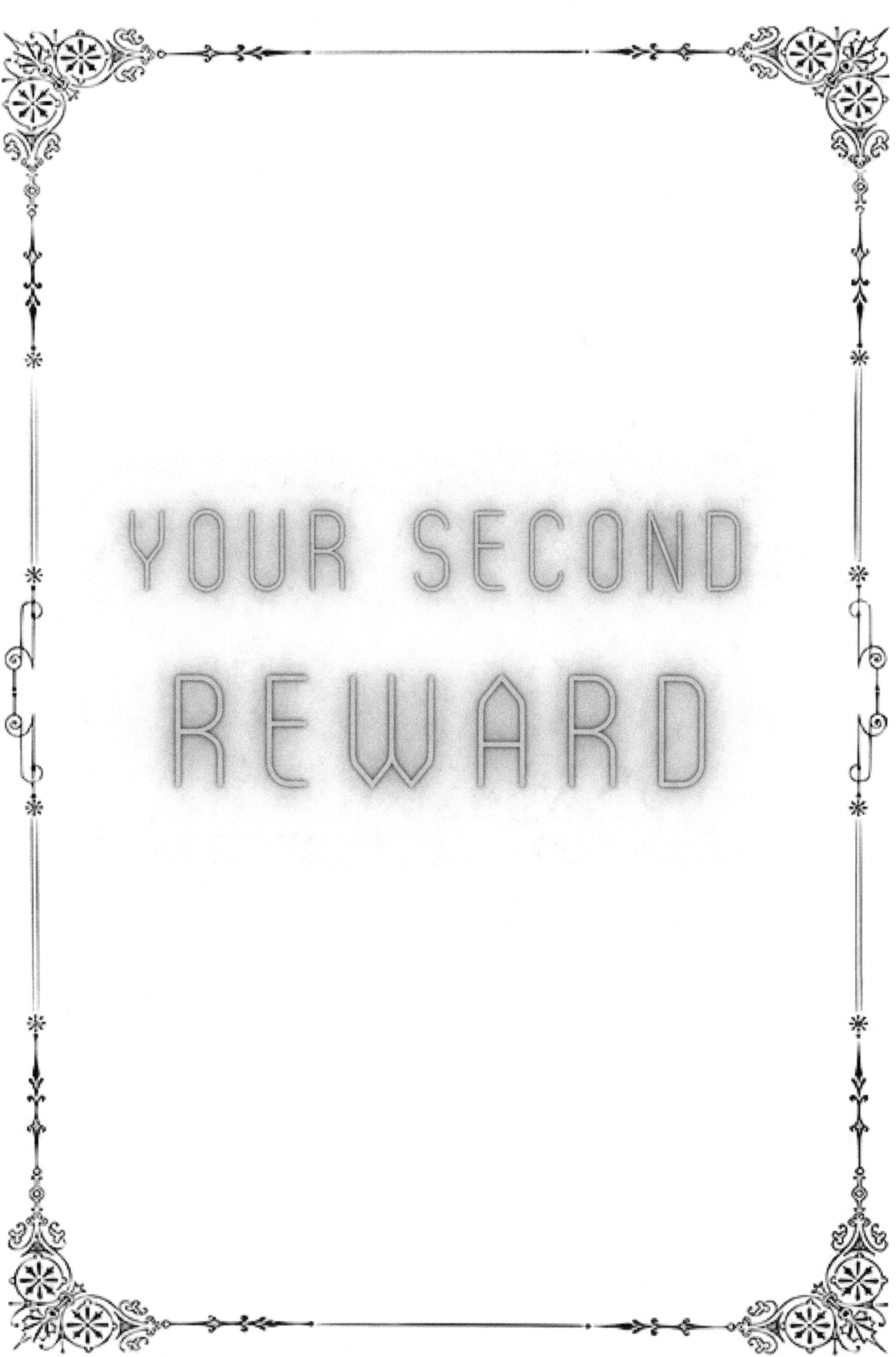

YOUR SECOND
REWARD

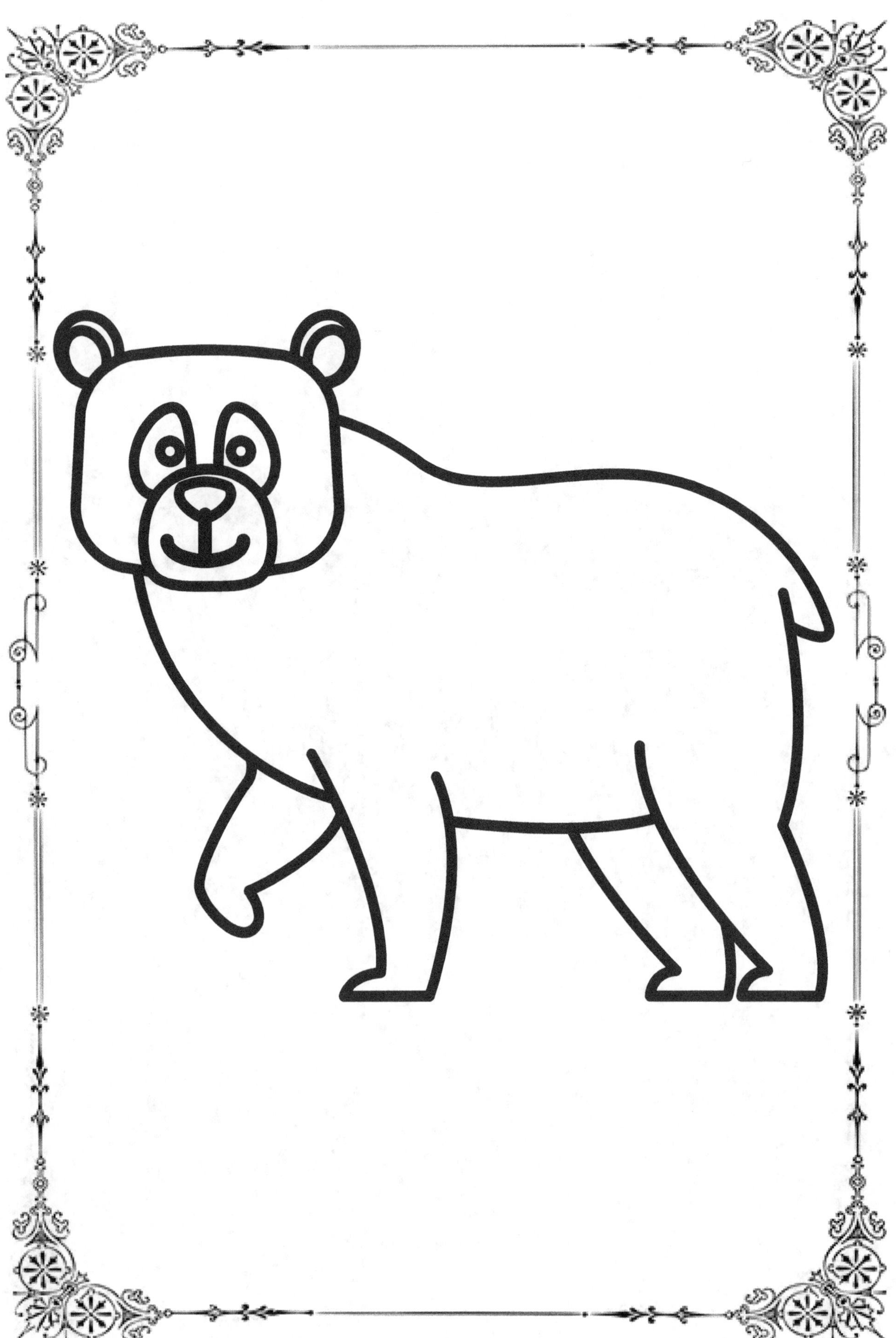

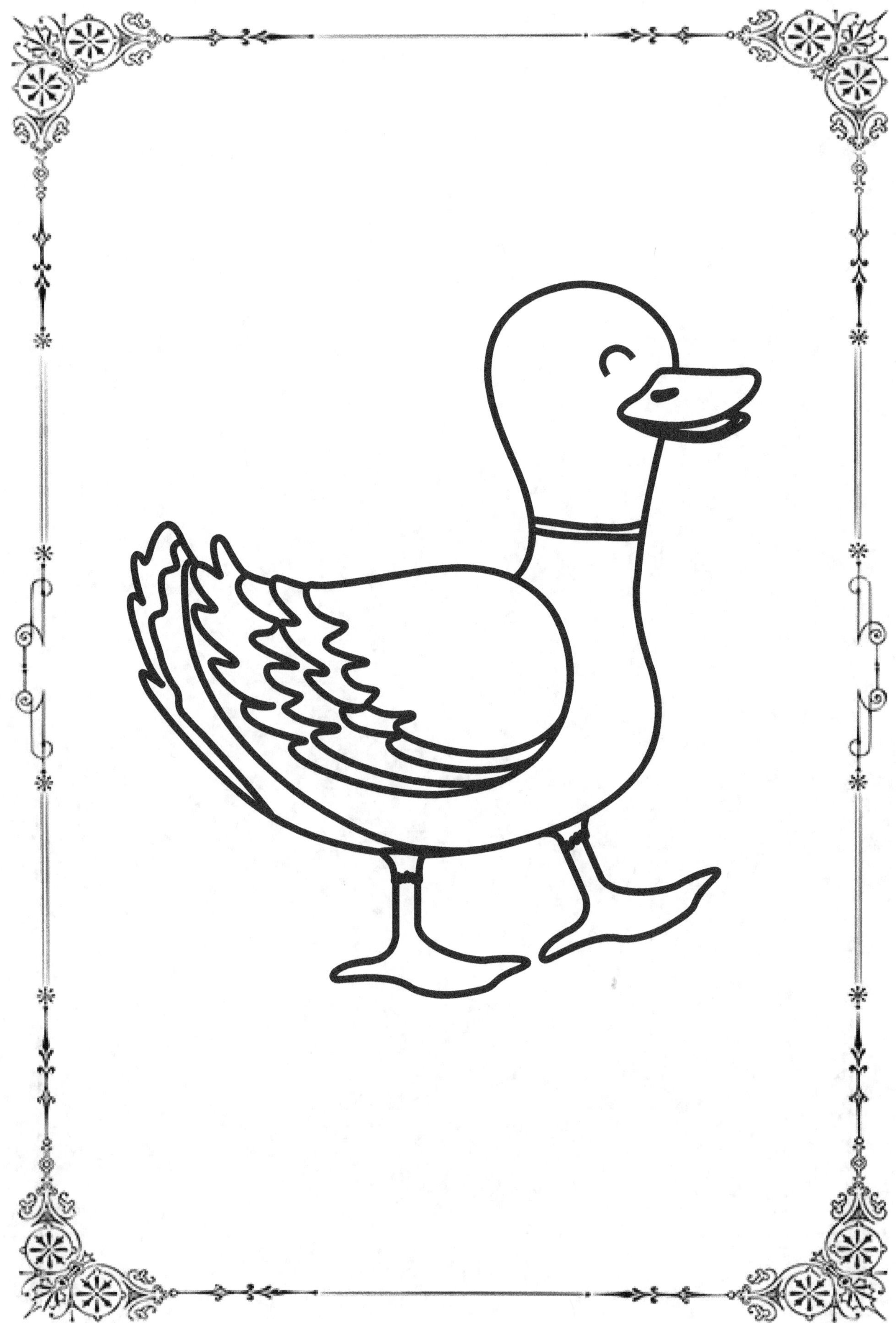

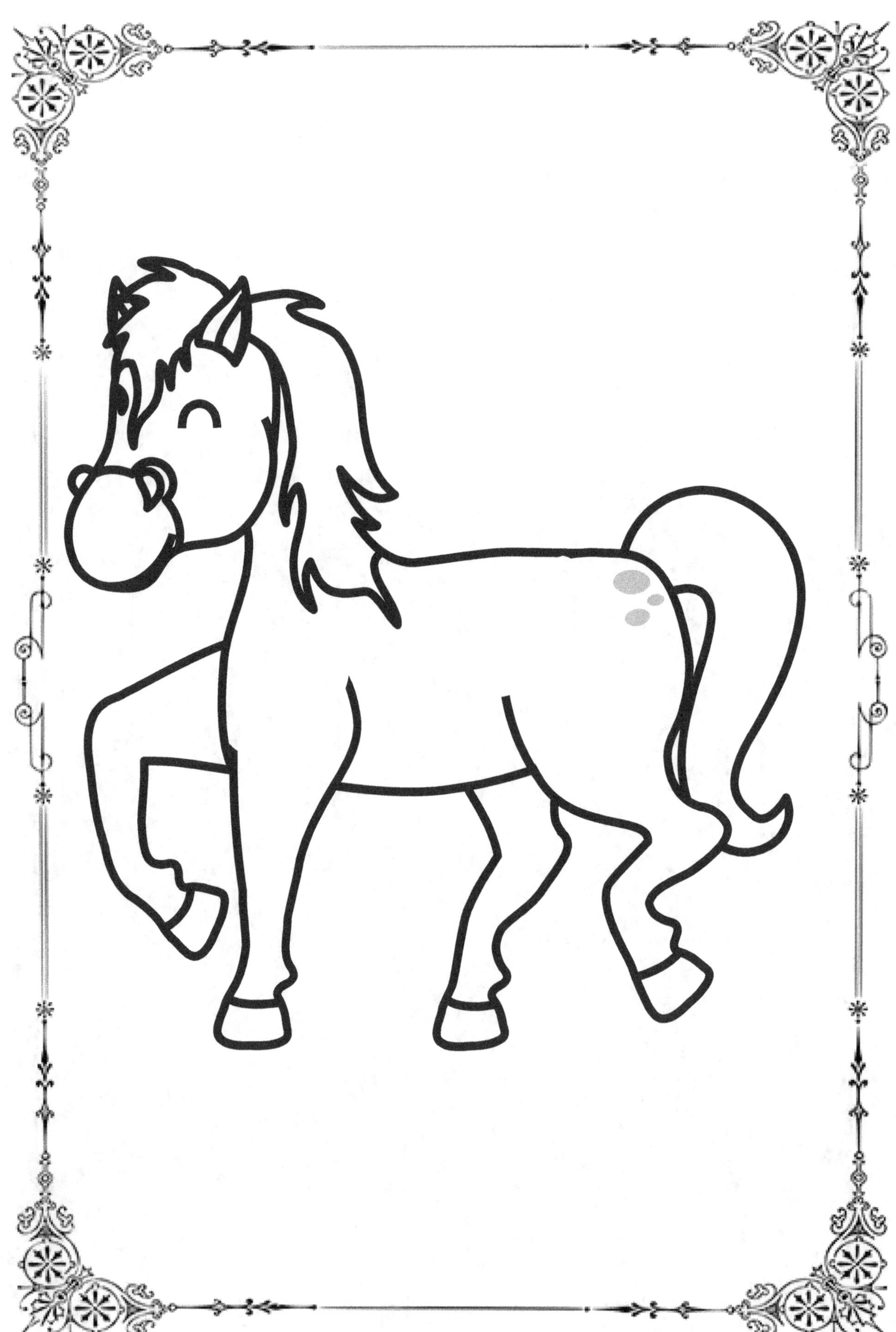

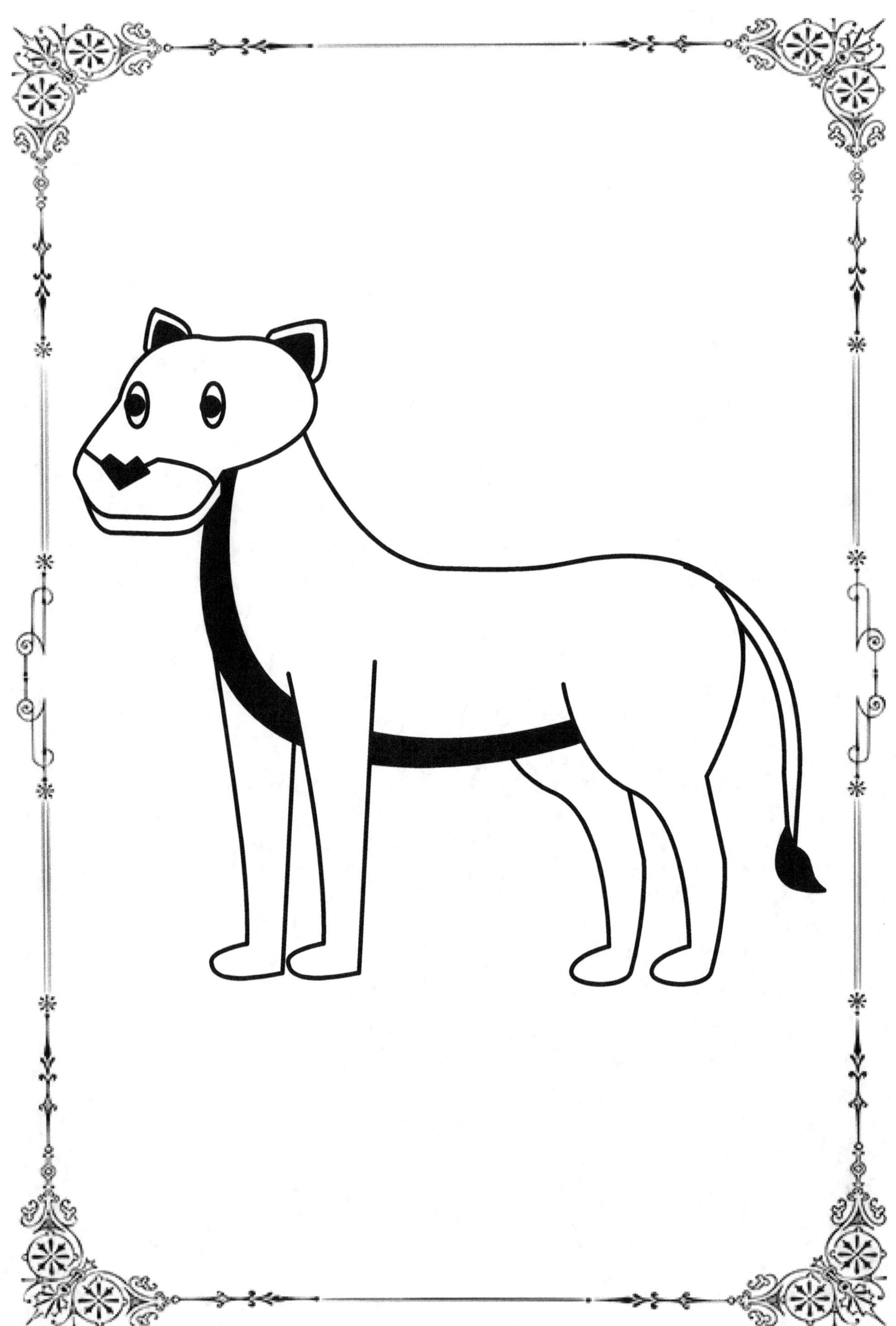

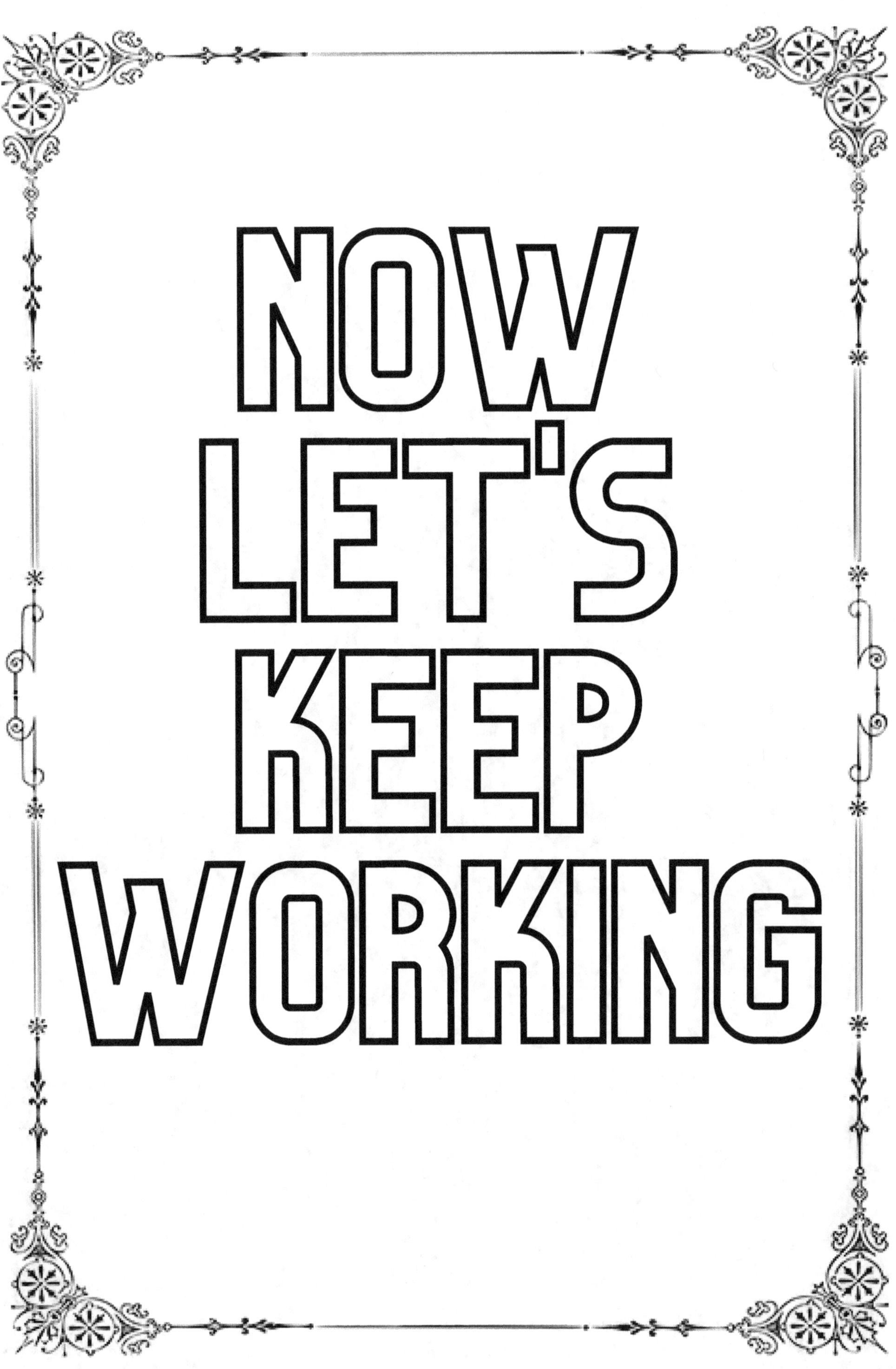

NOW
LET'S
KEEP
WORKING

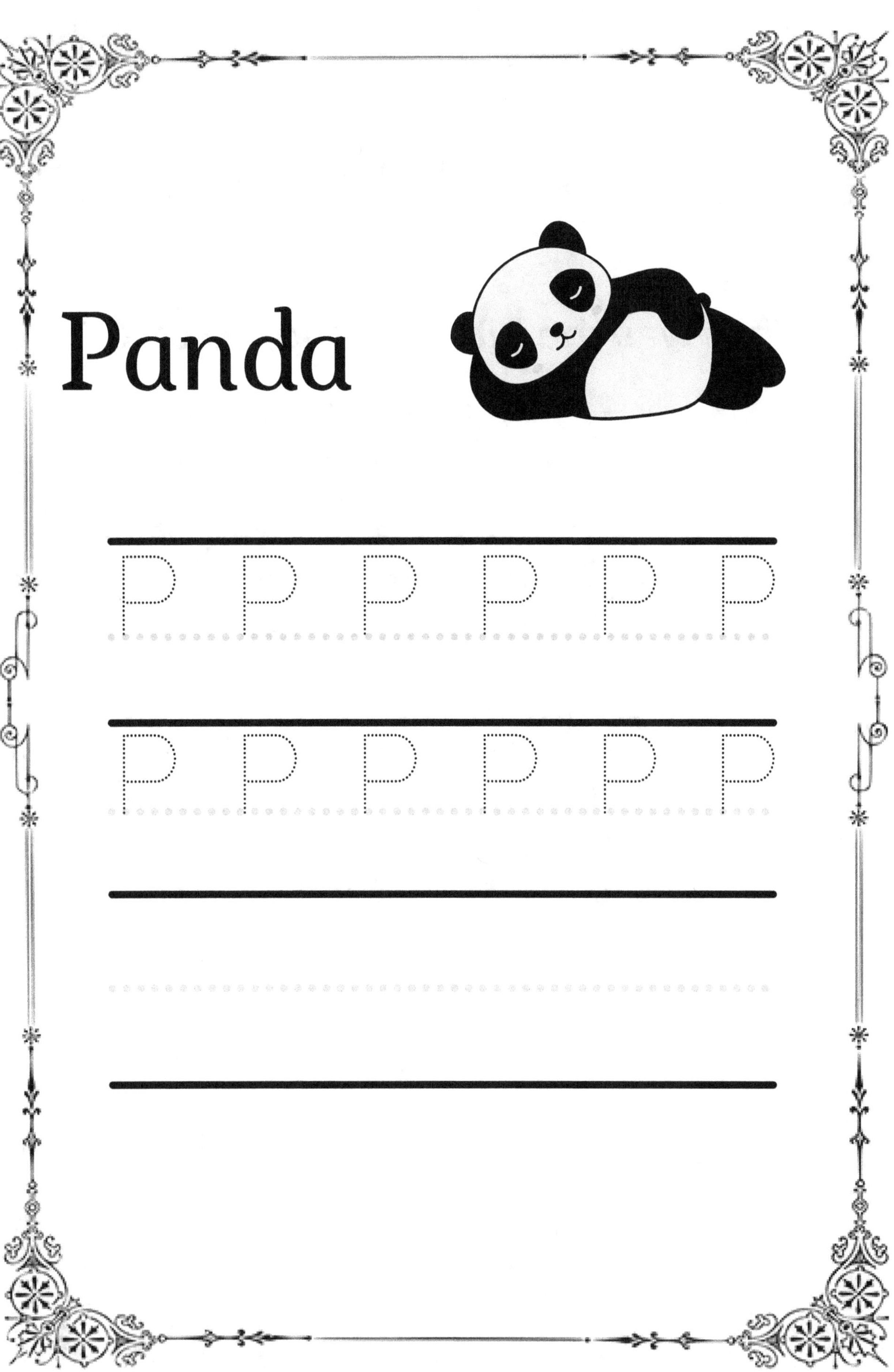

Panda

What was the kitten's favorite color?
Purrr-ple!

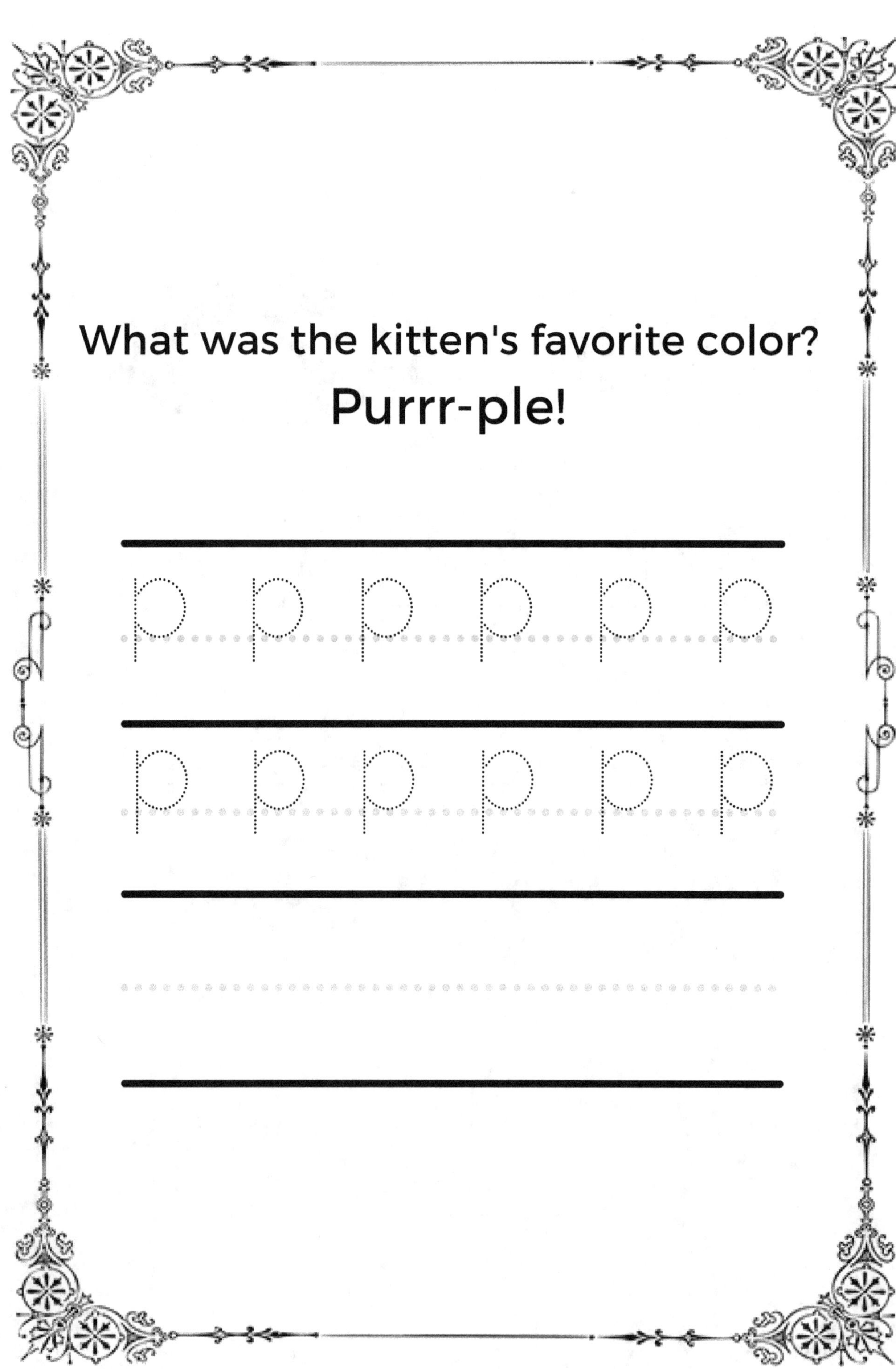

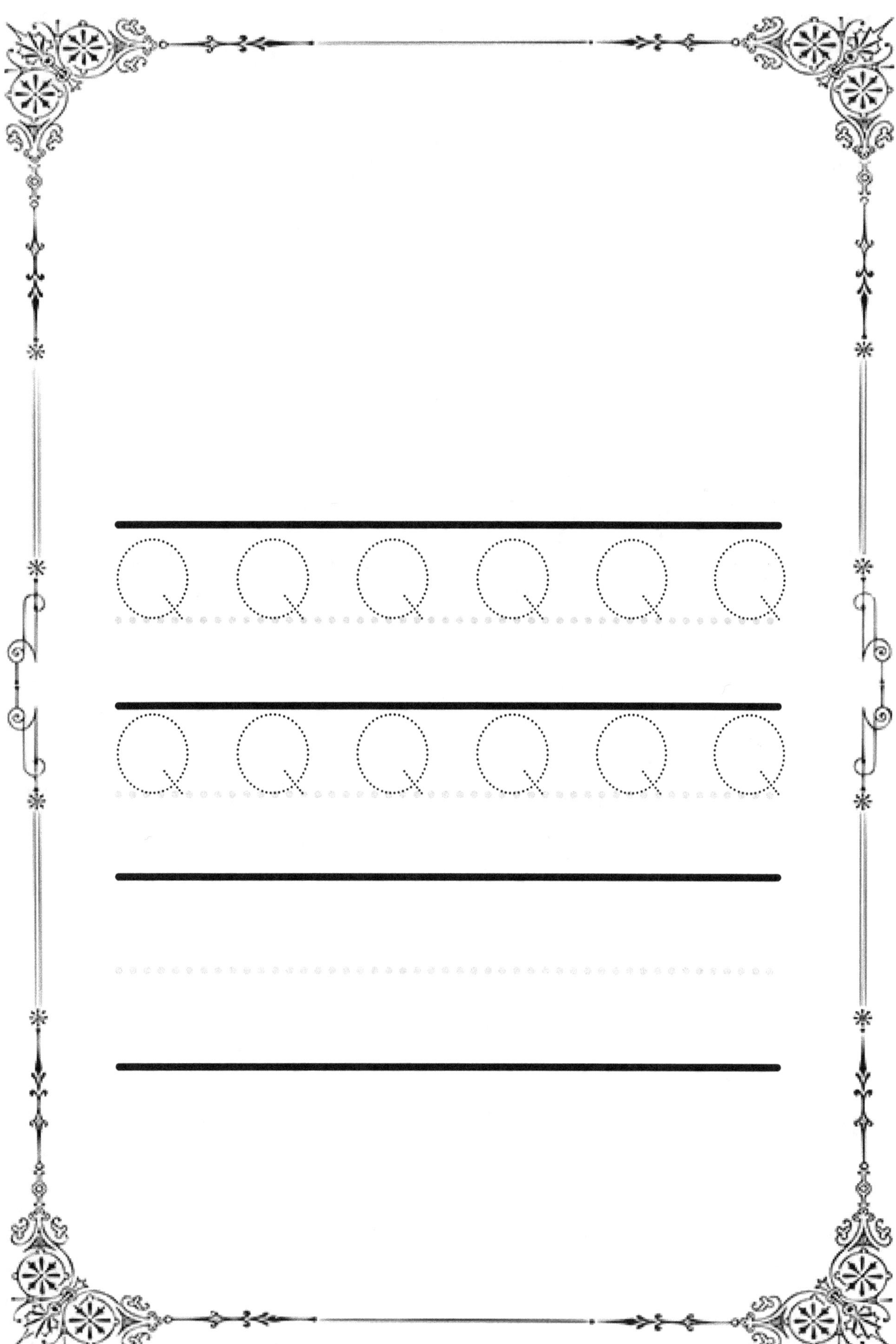

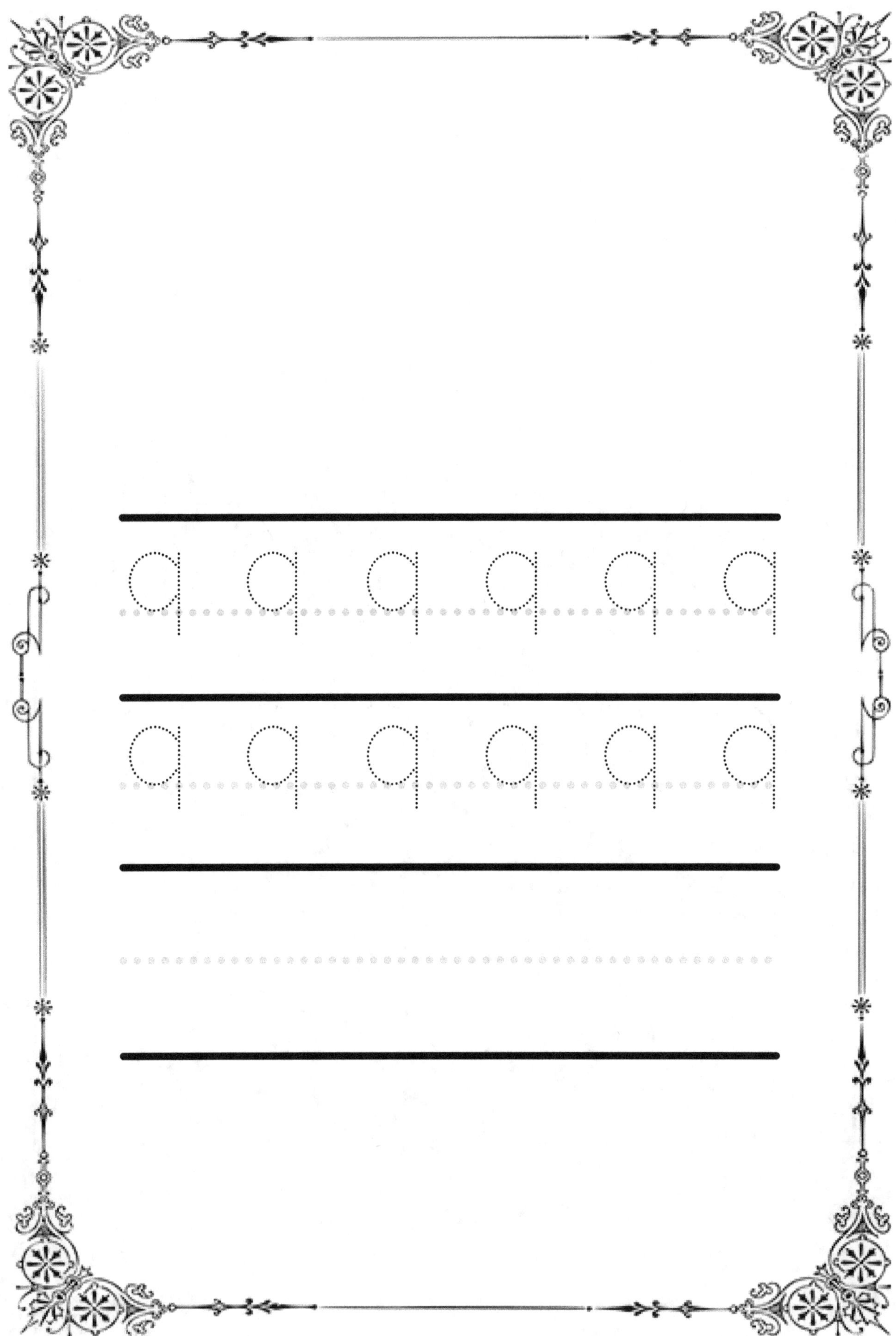

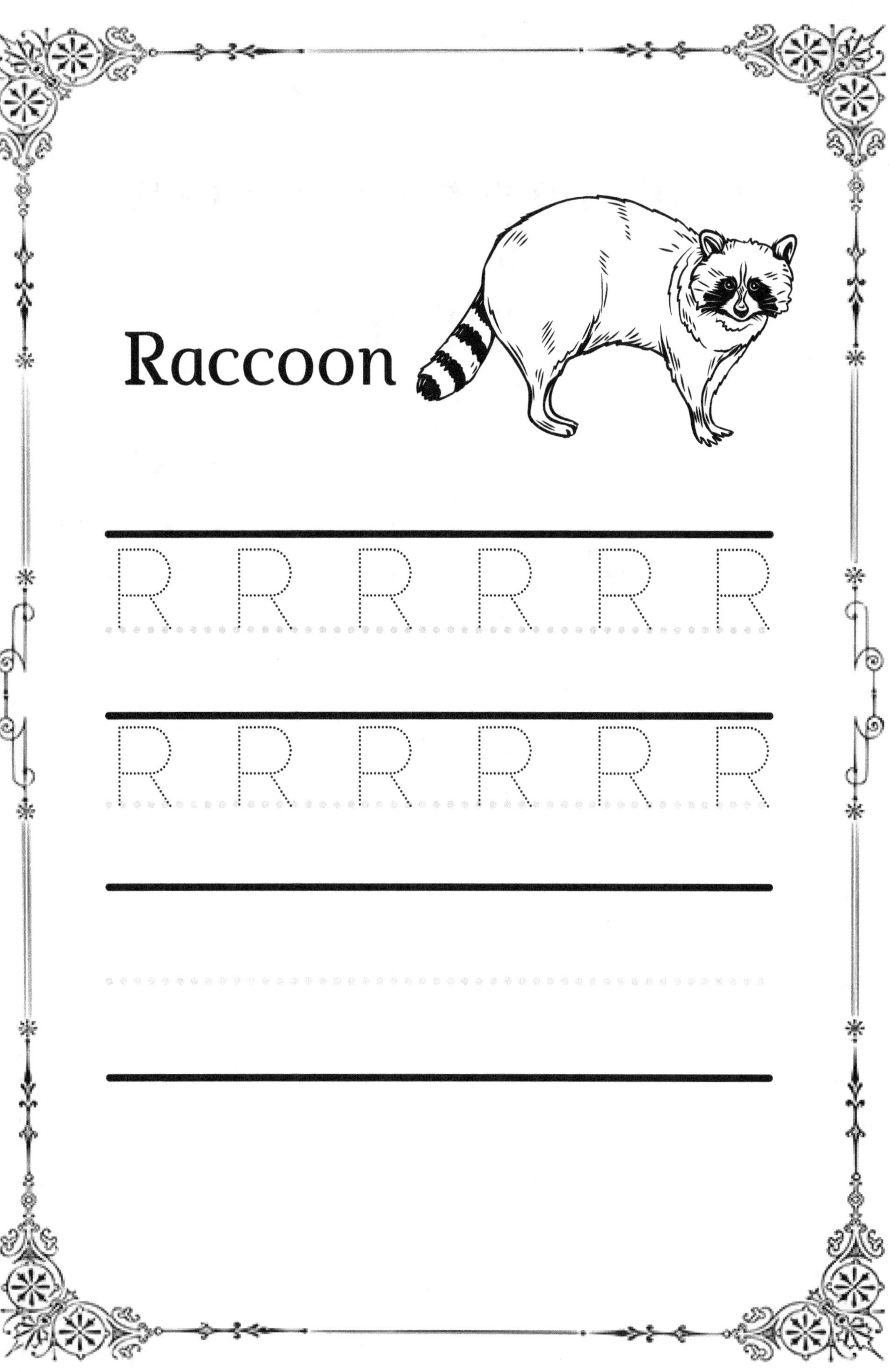

Raccoon
R R R R R R
R R R R R R

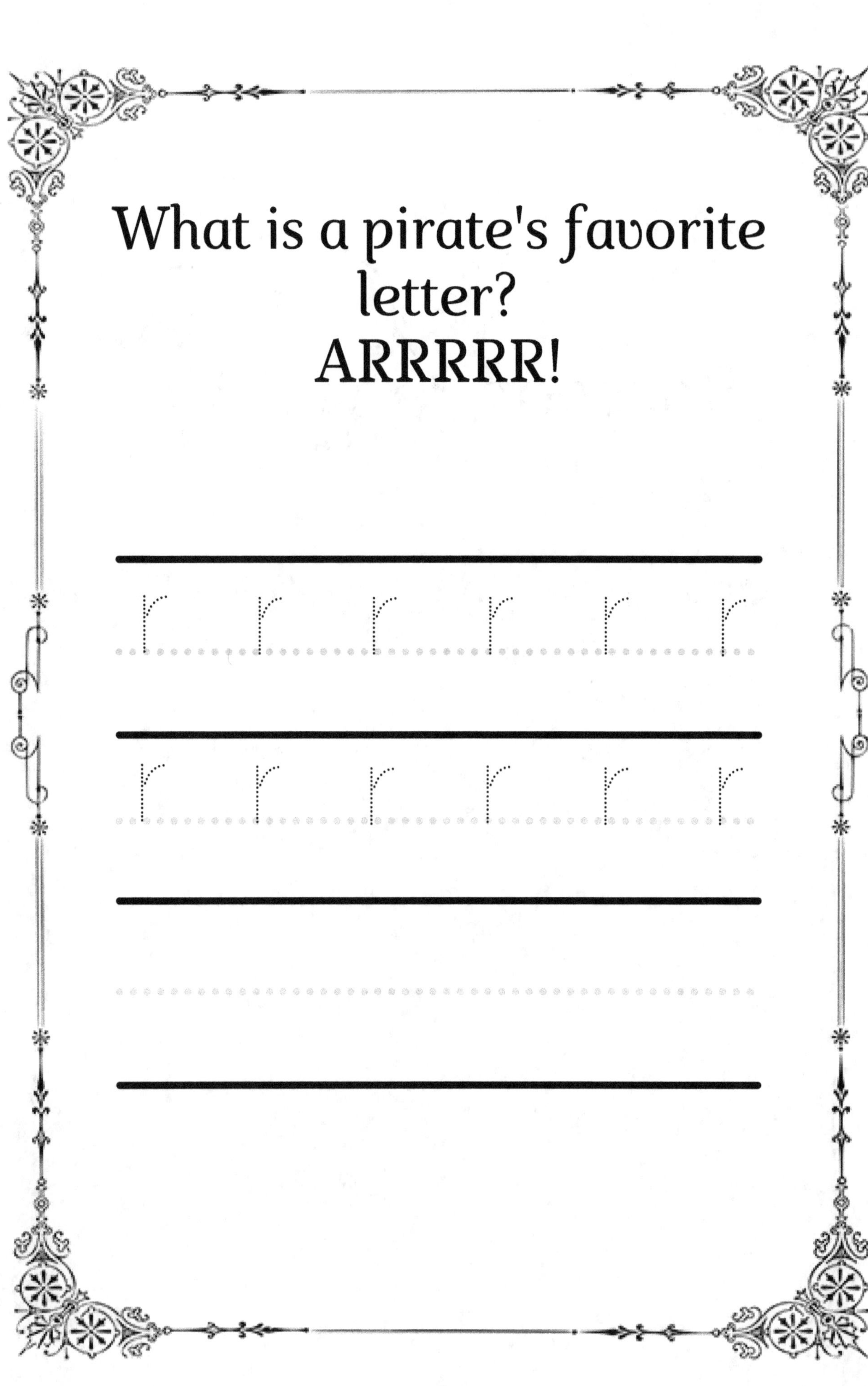

What is a pirate's favorite letter?
ARRRRR!

Snake

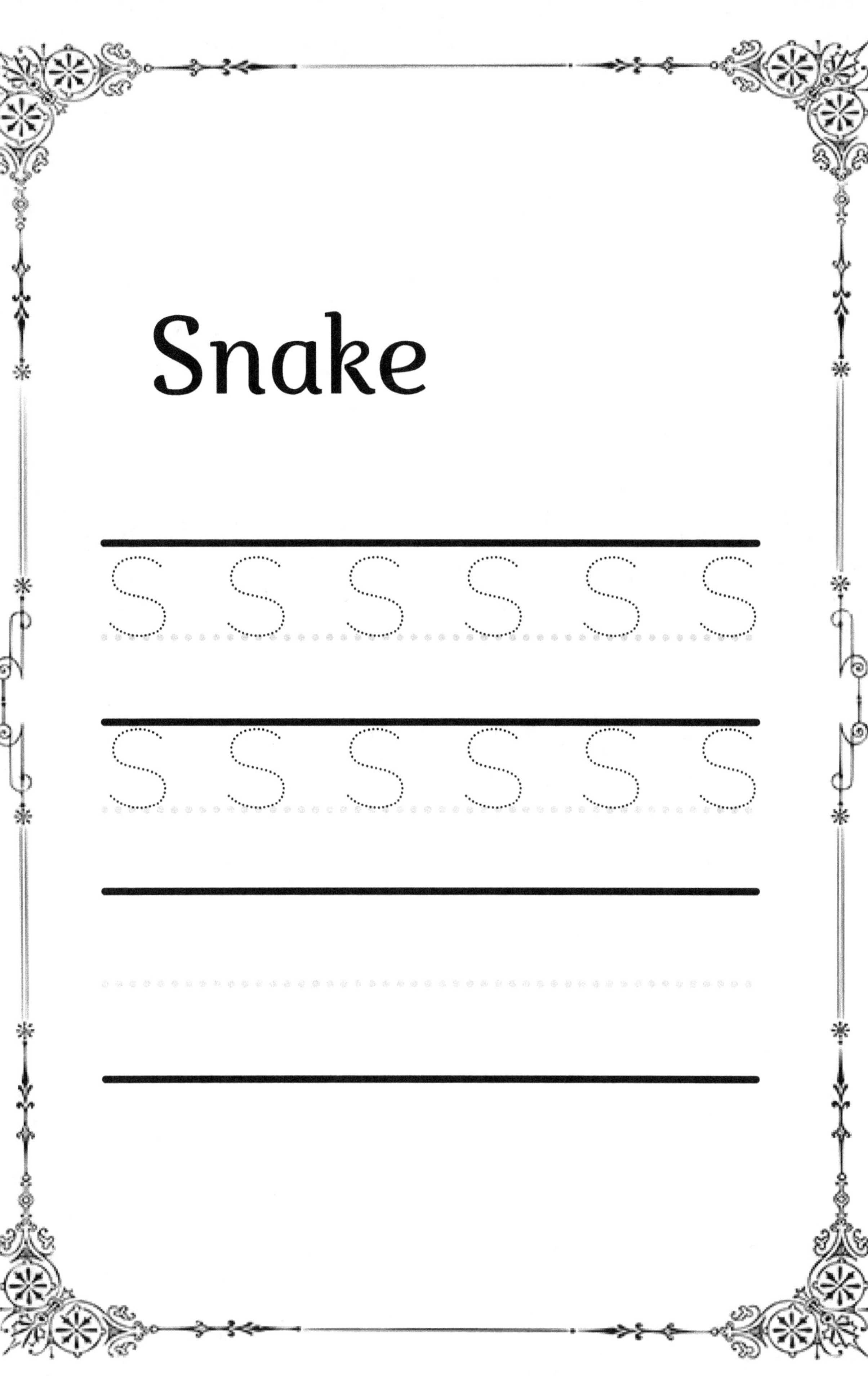

Tiger

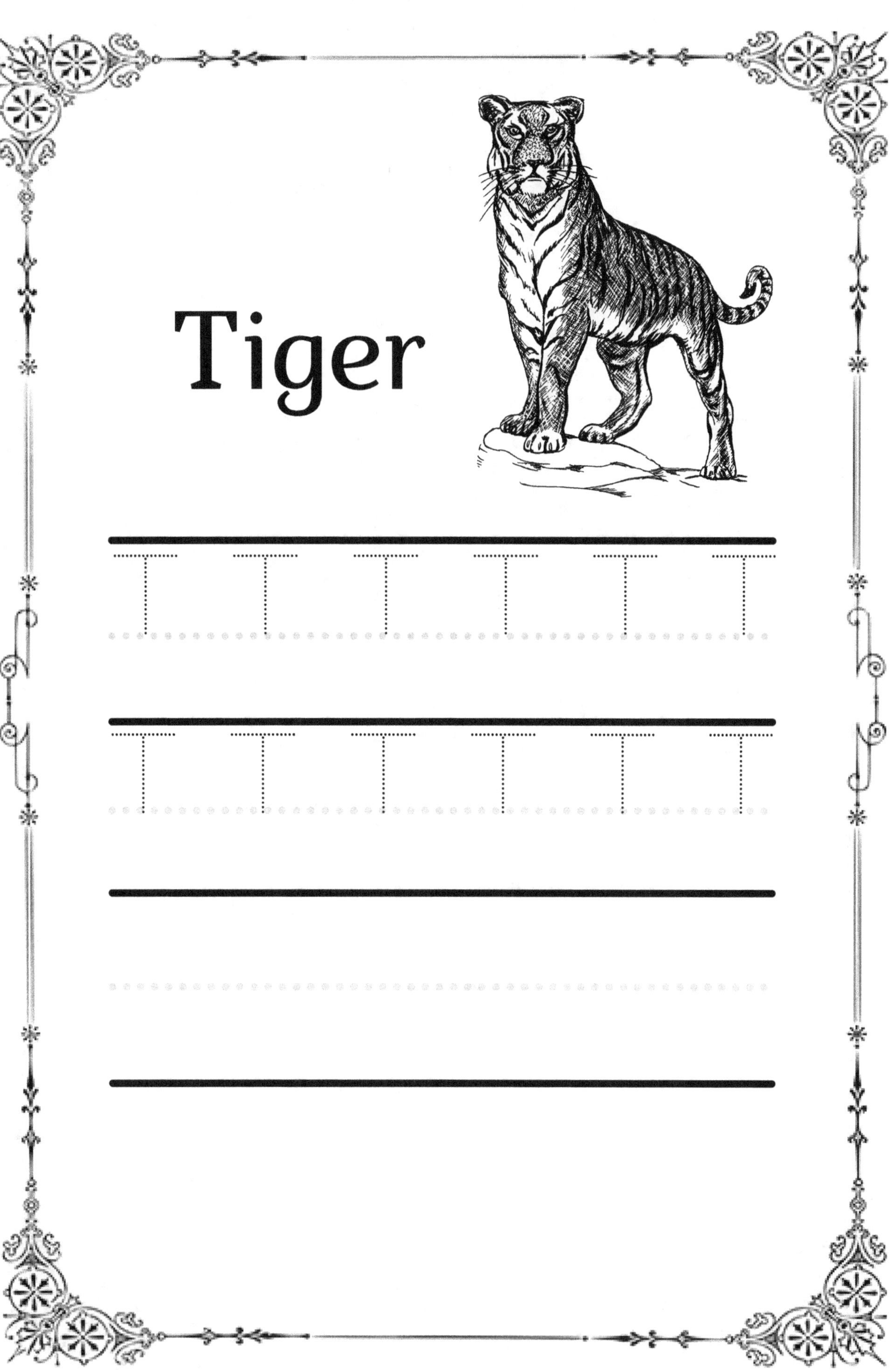

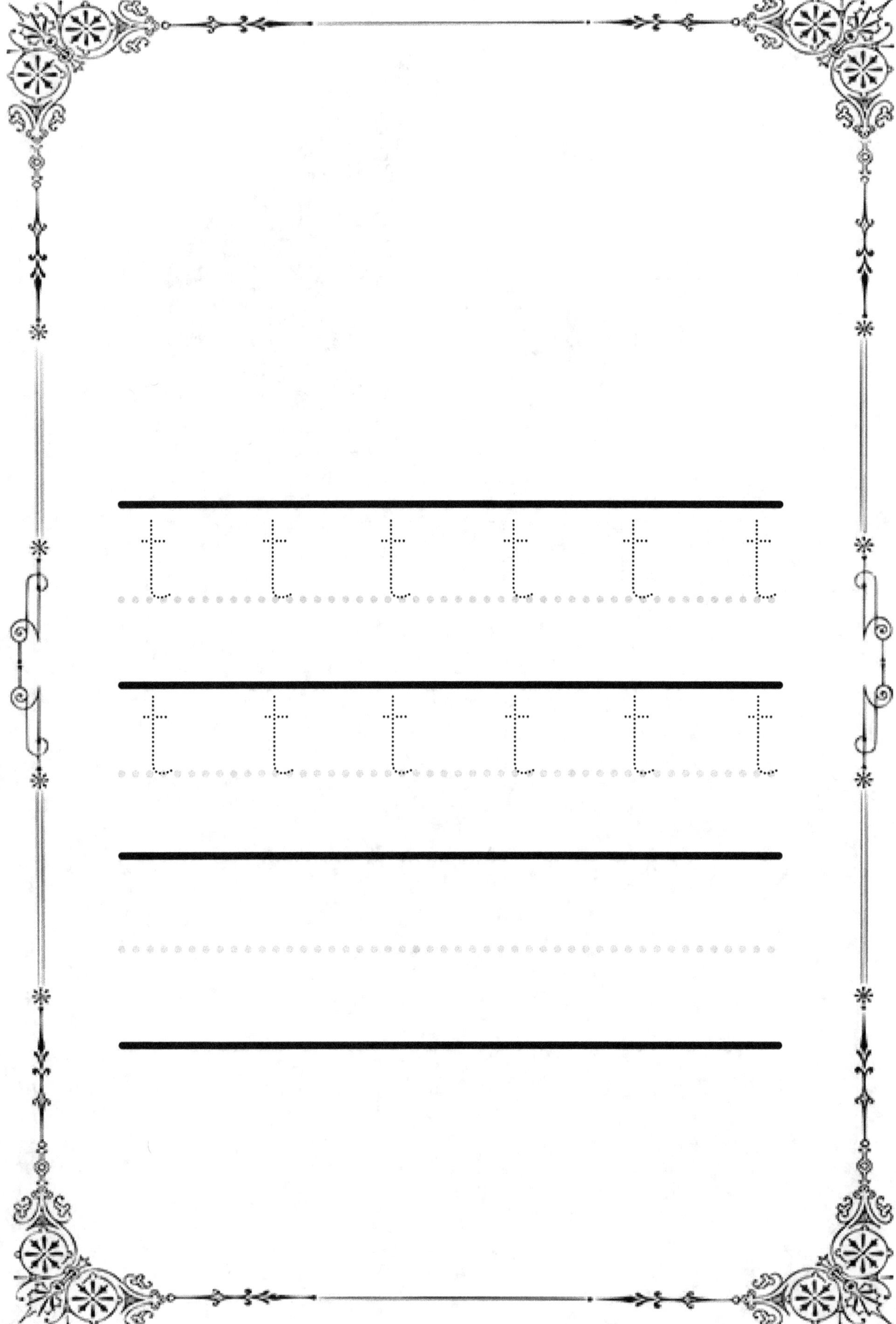

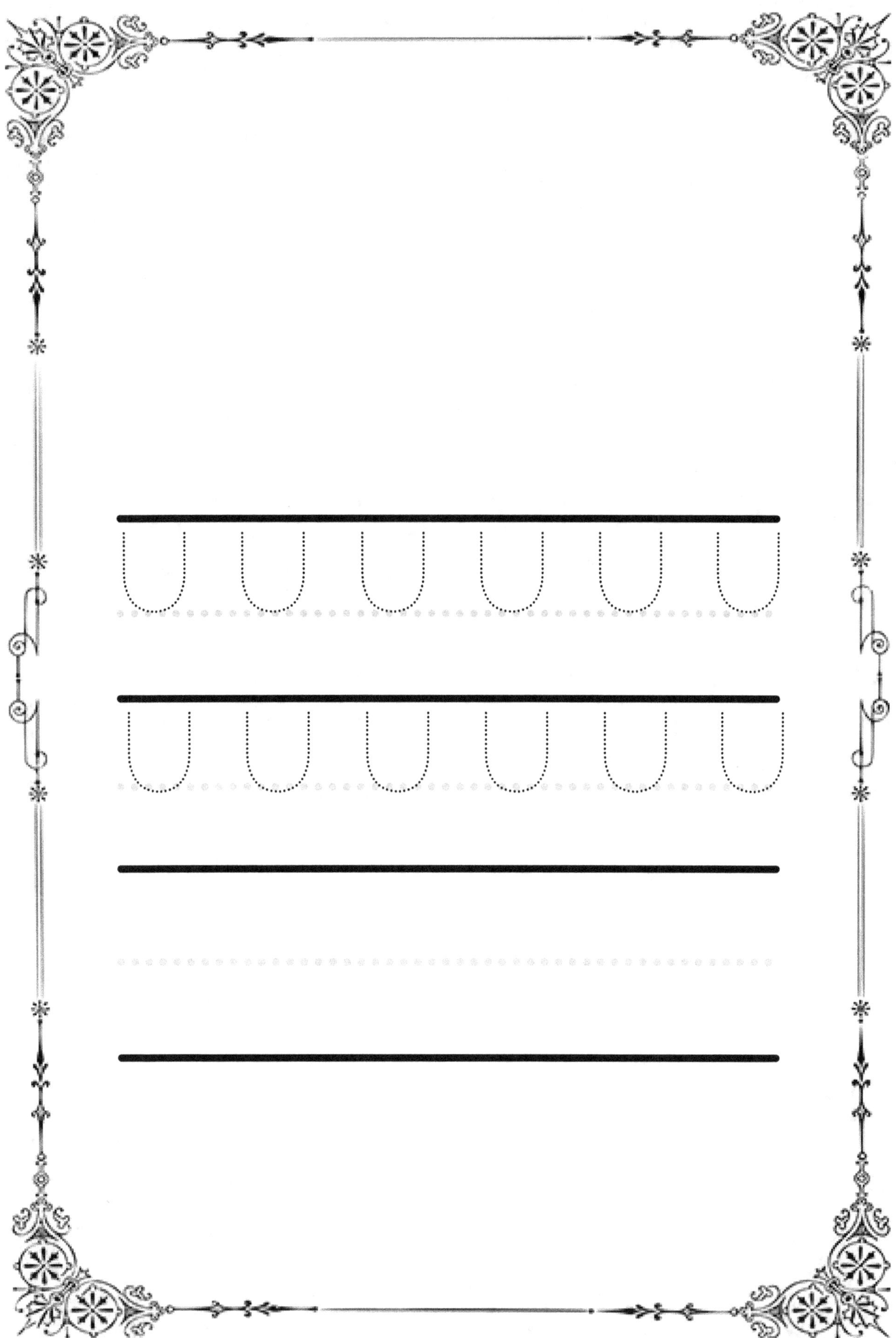

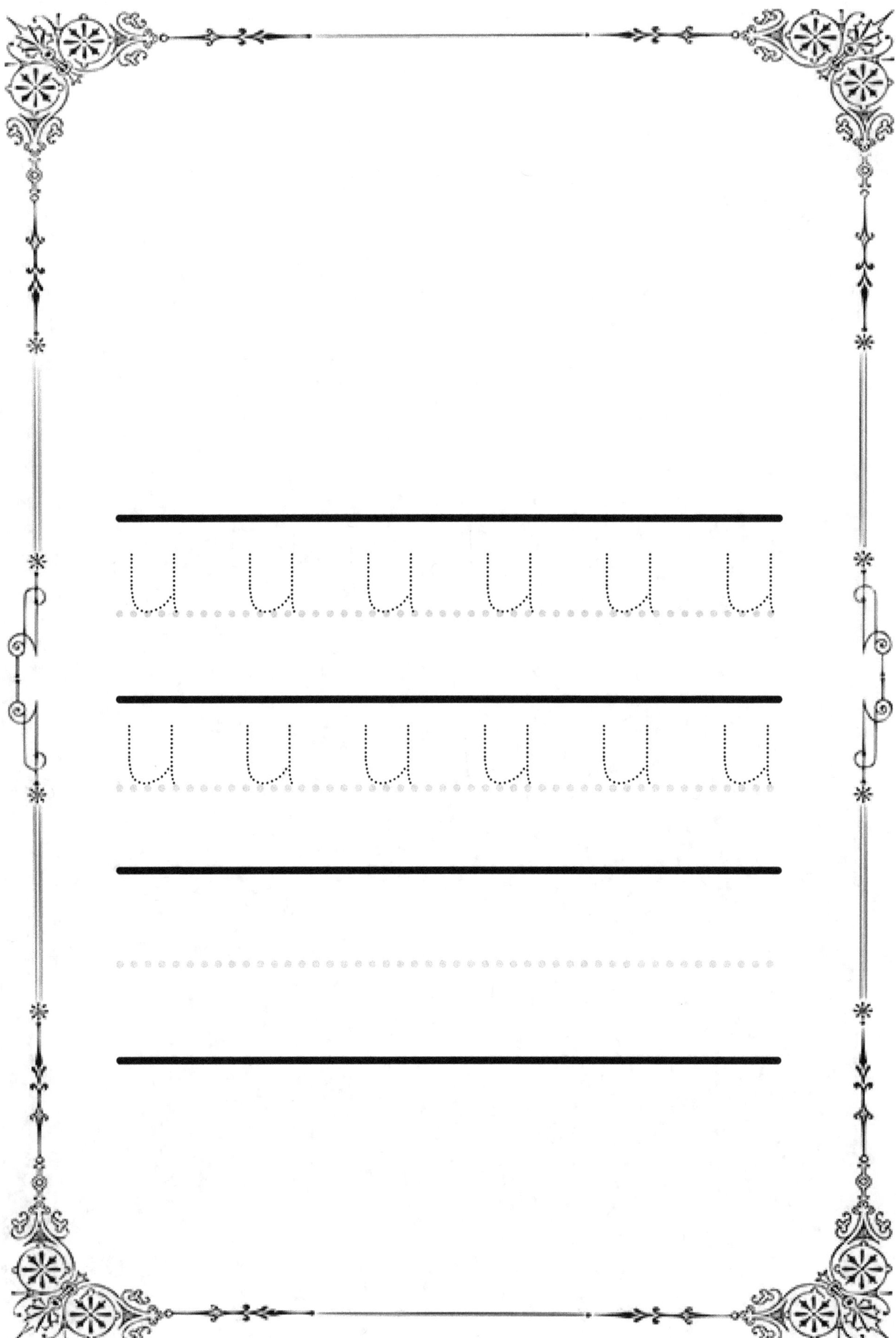

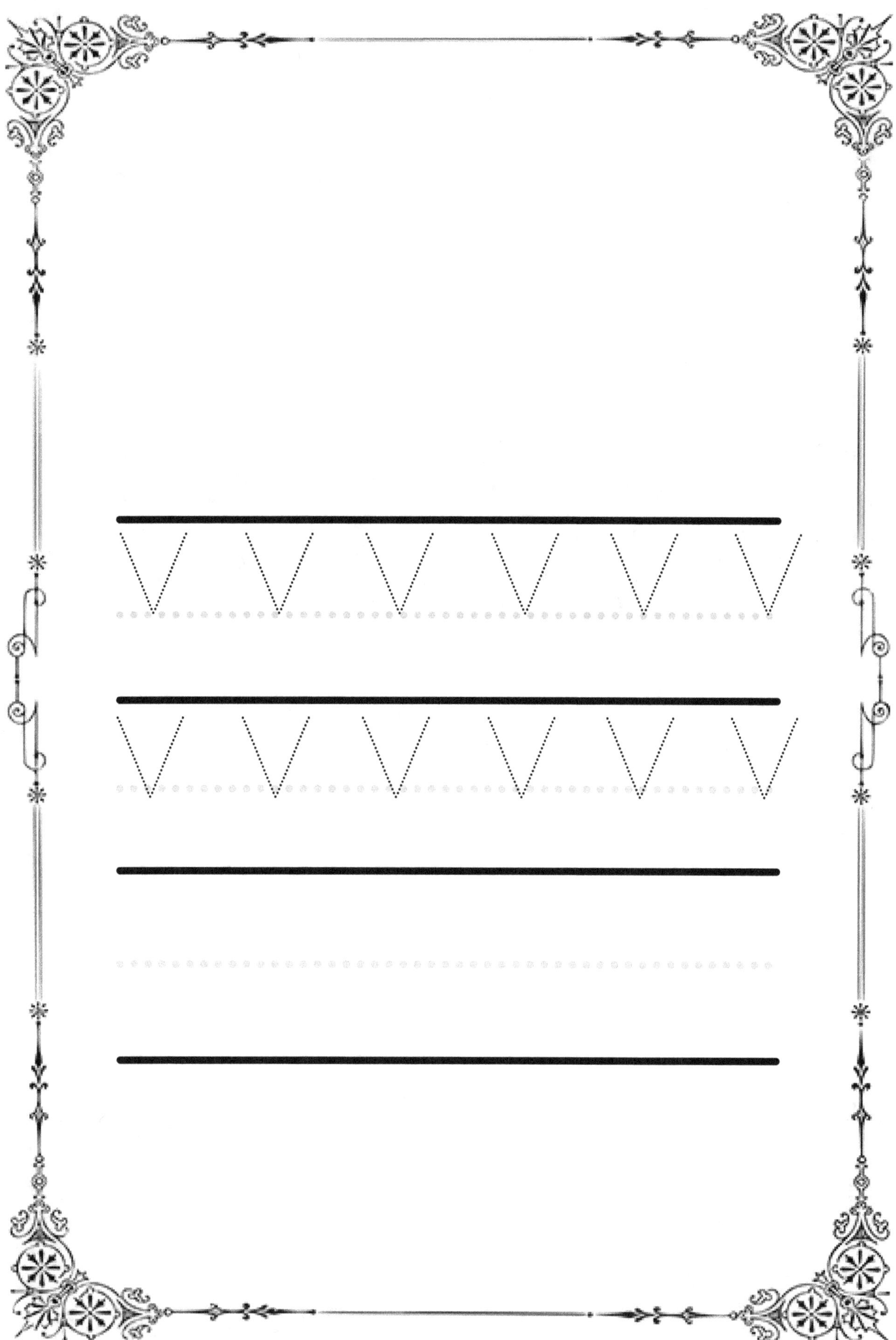

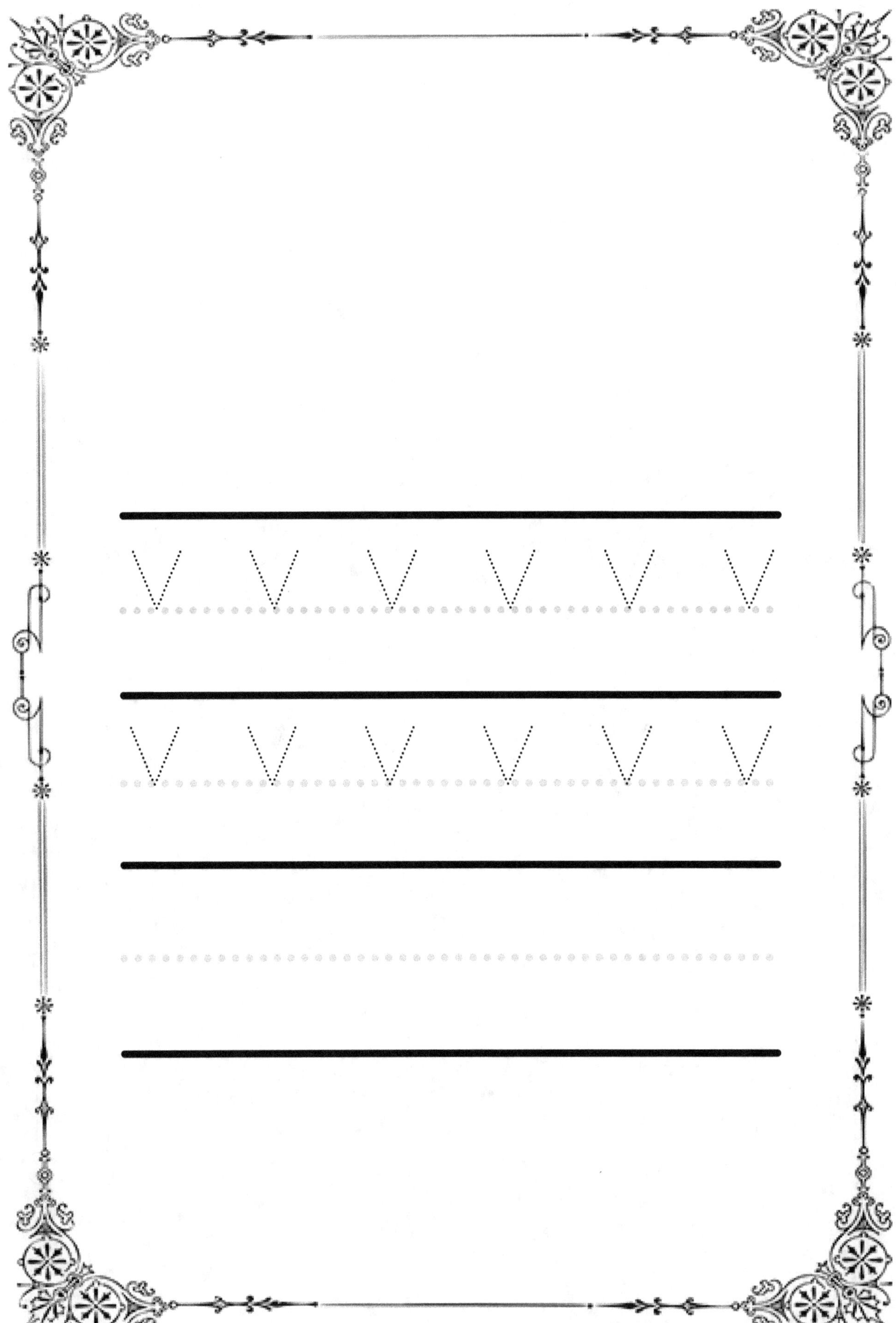

Wolf

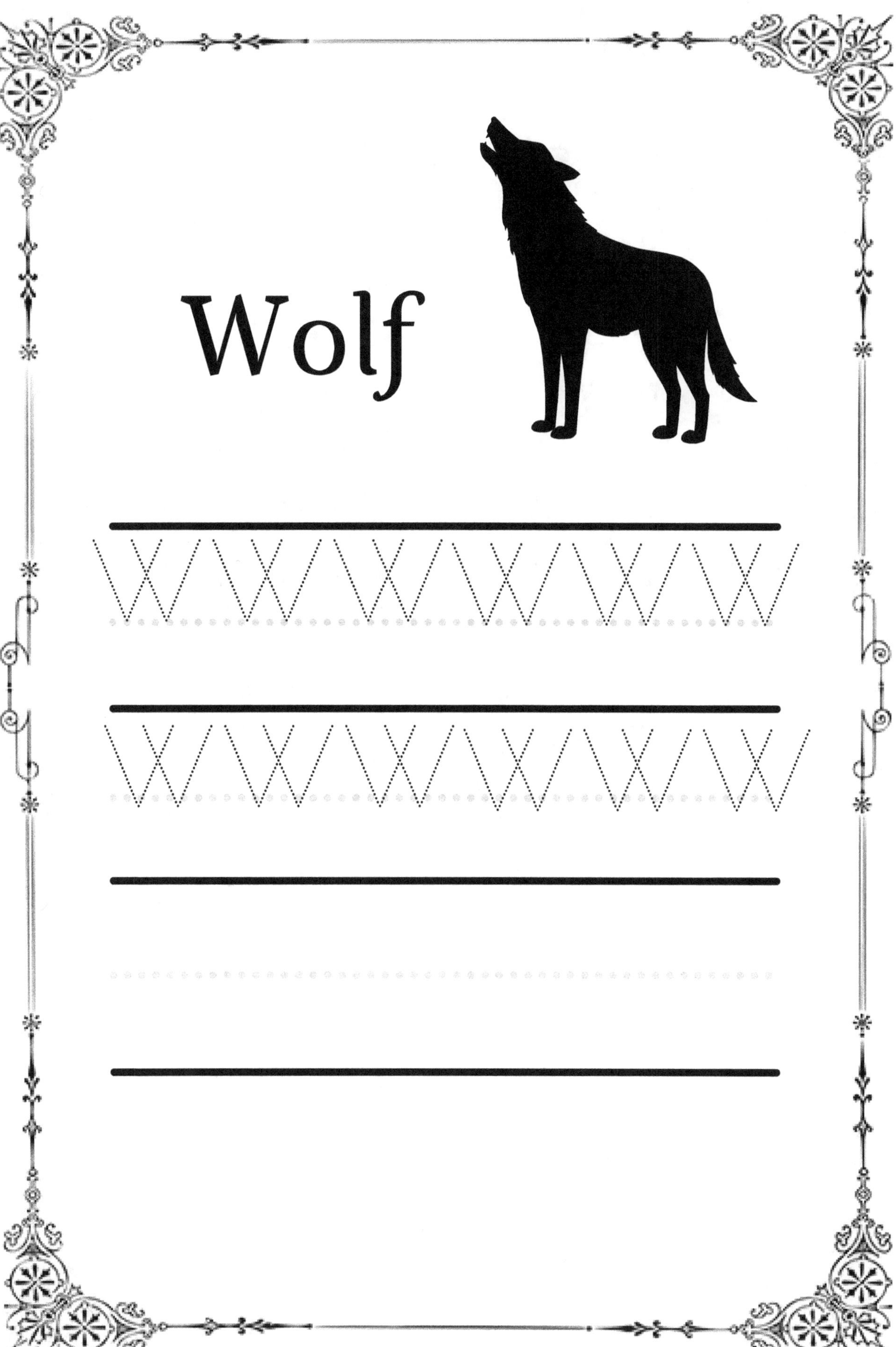

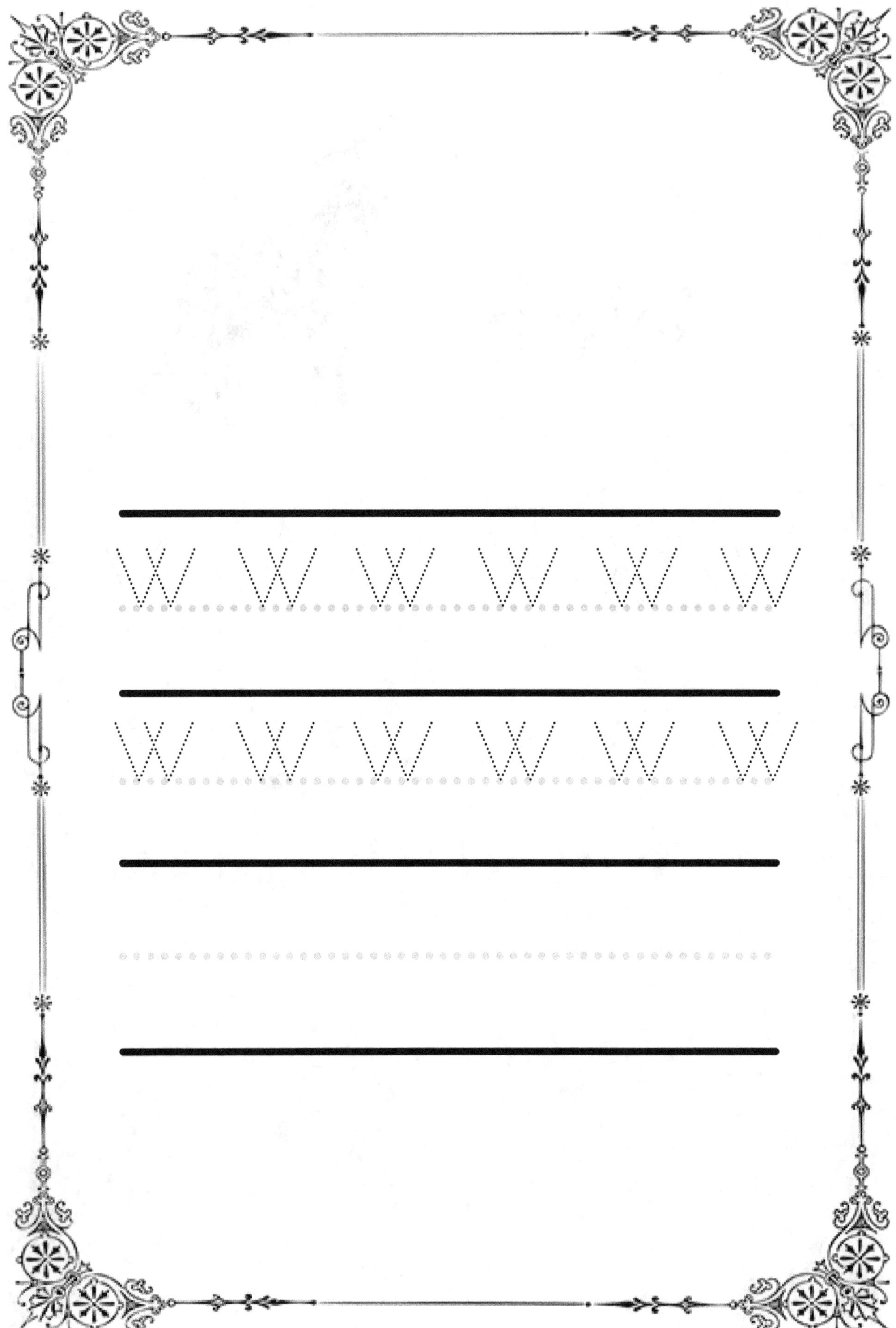

What is a pirate's favorite letter?
ARRRRR!

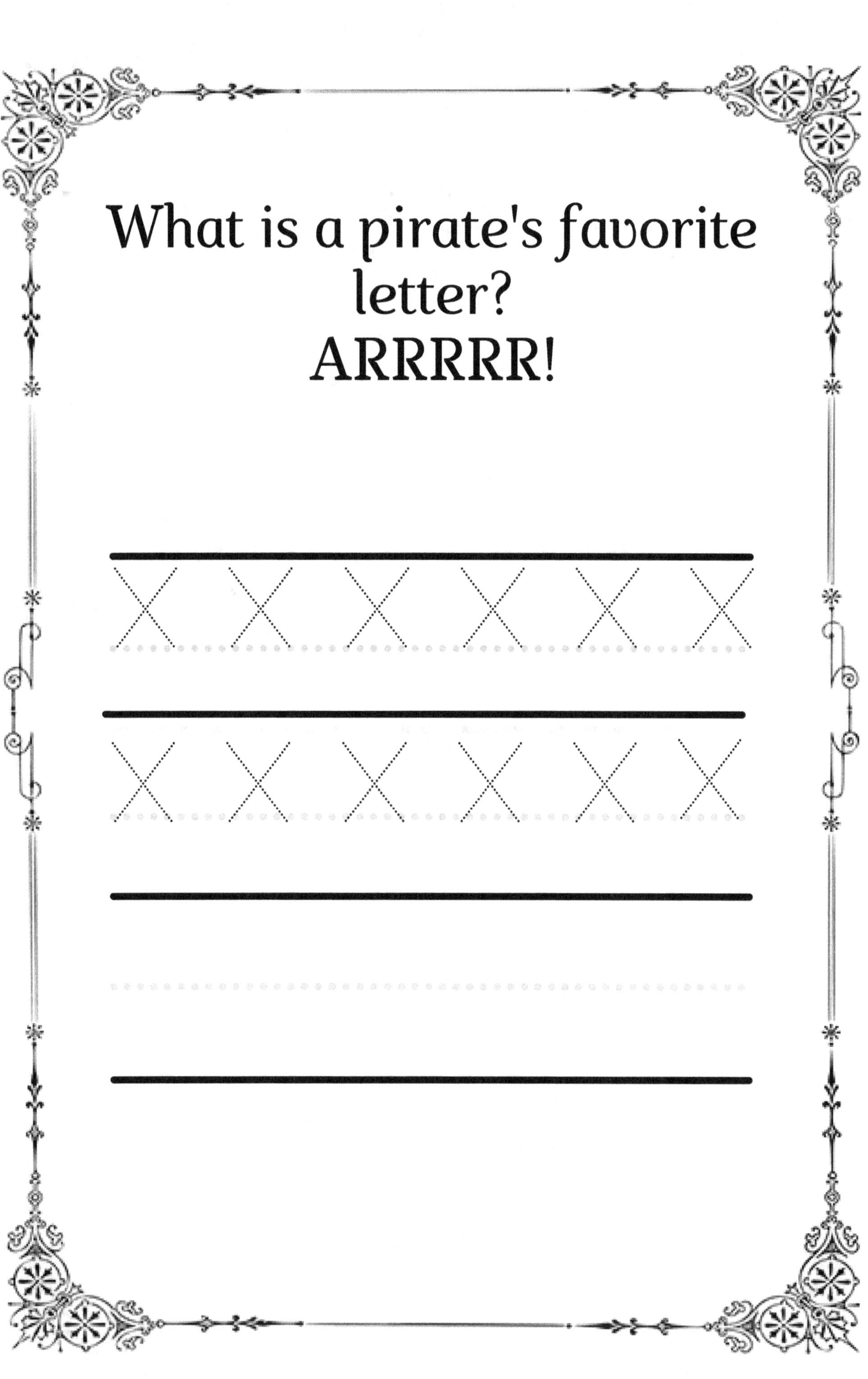

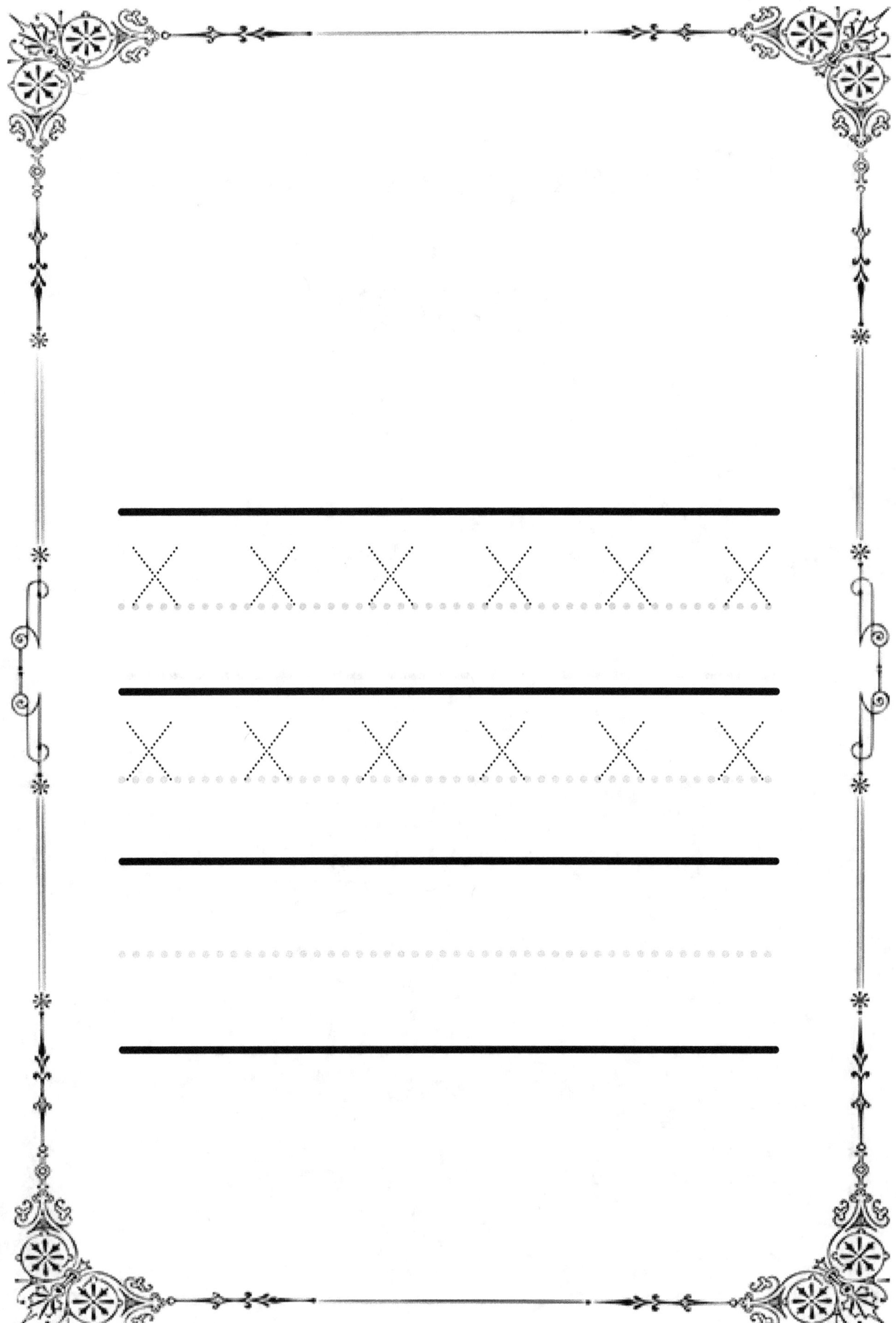

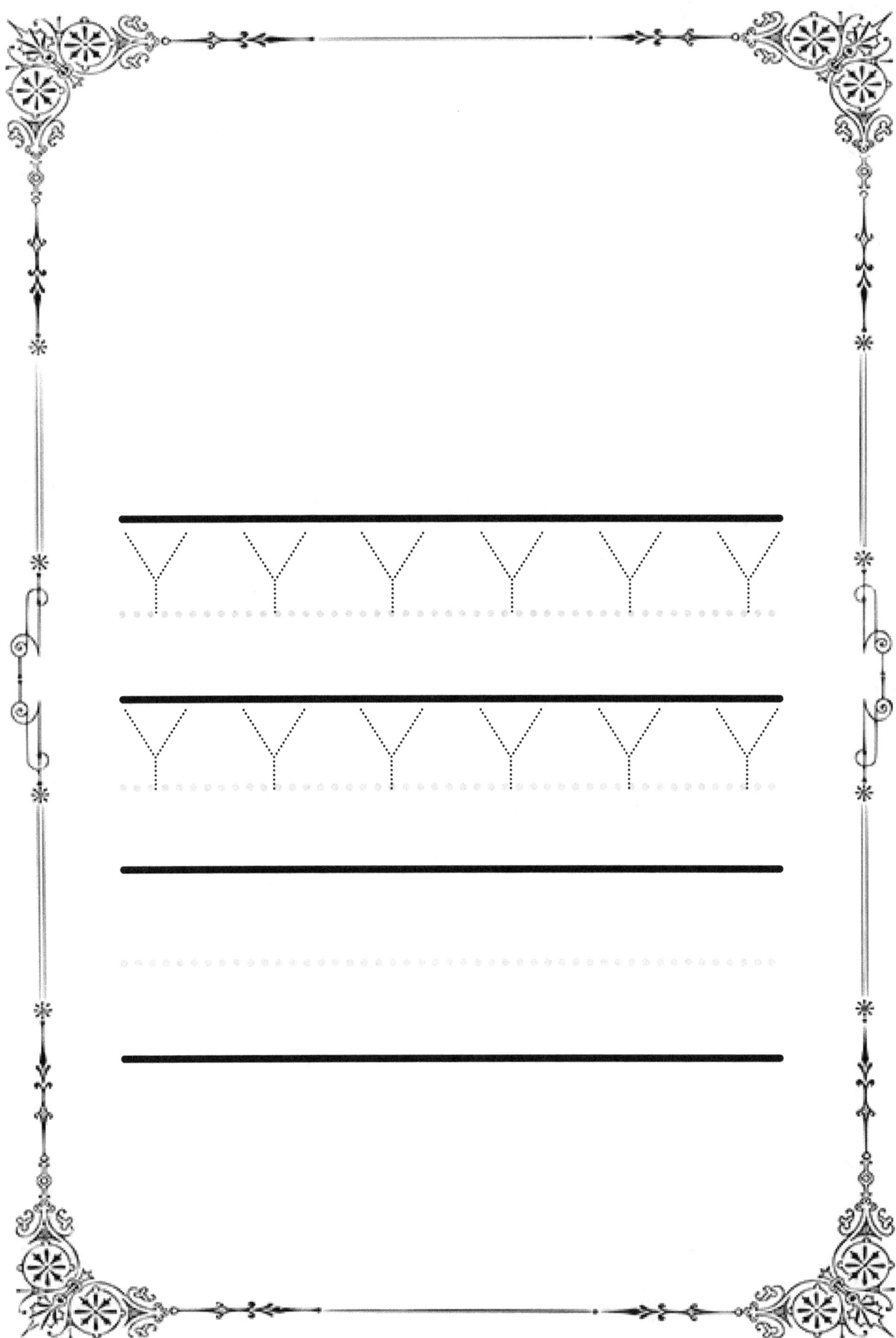

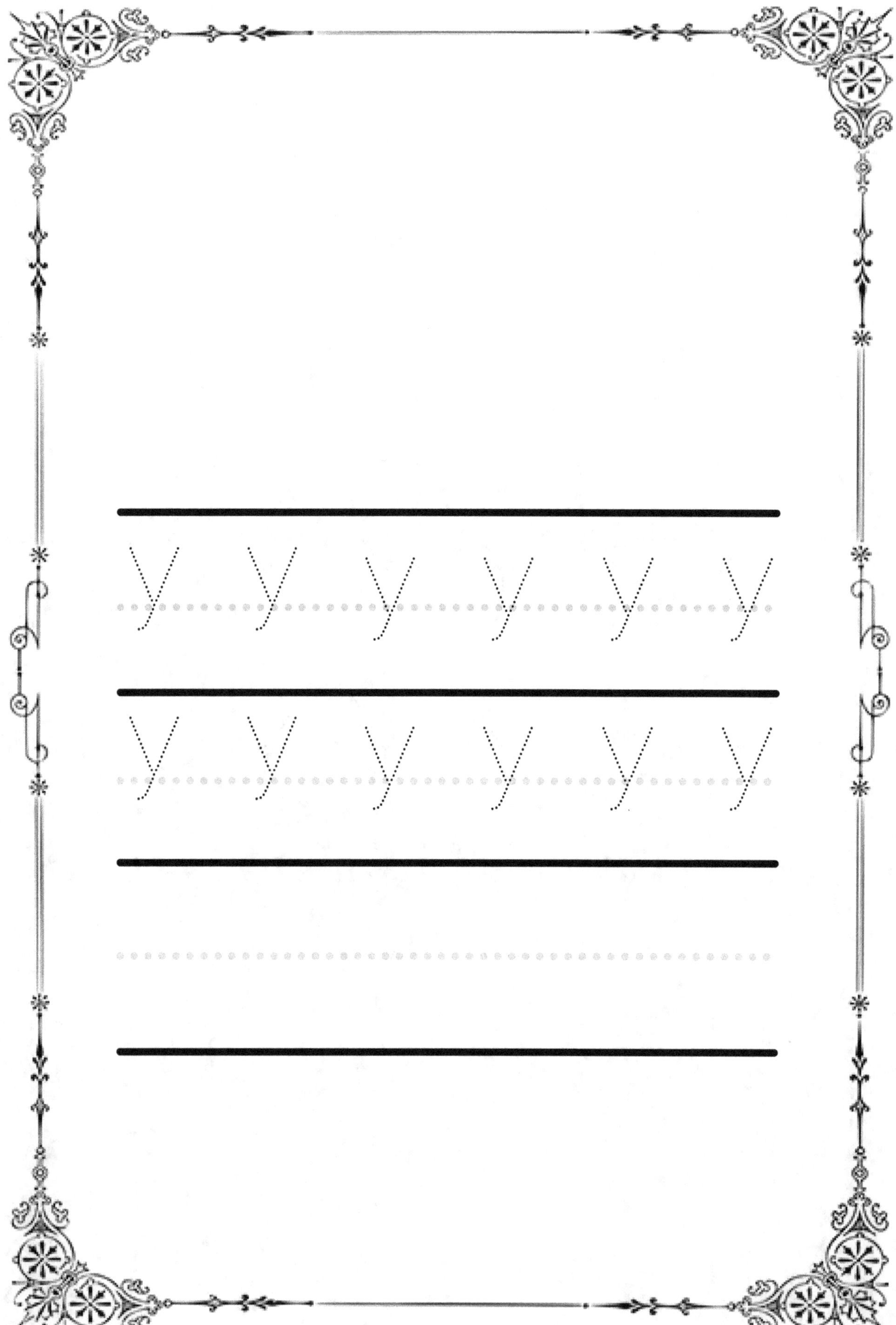

y   y   y   y   y   y
y   y   y   y   y   y

Zebra

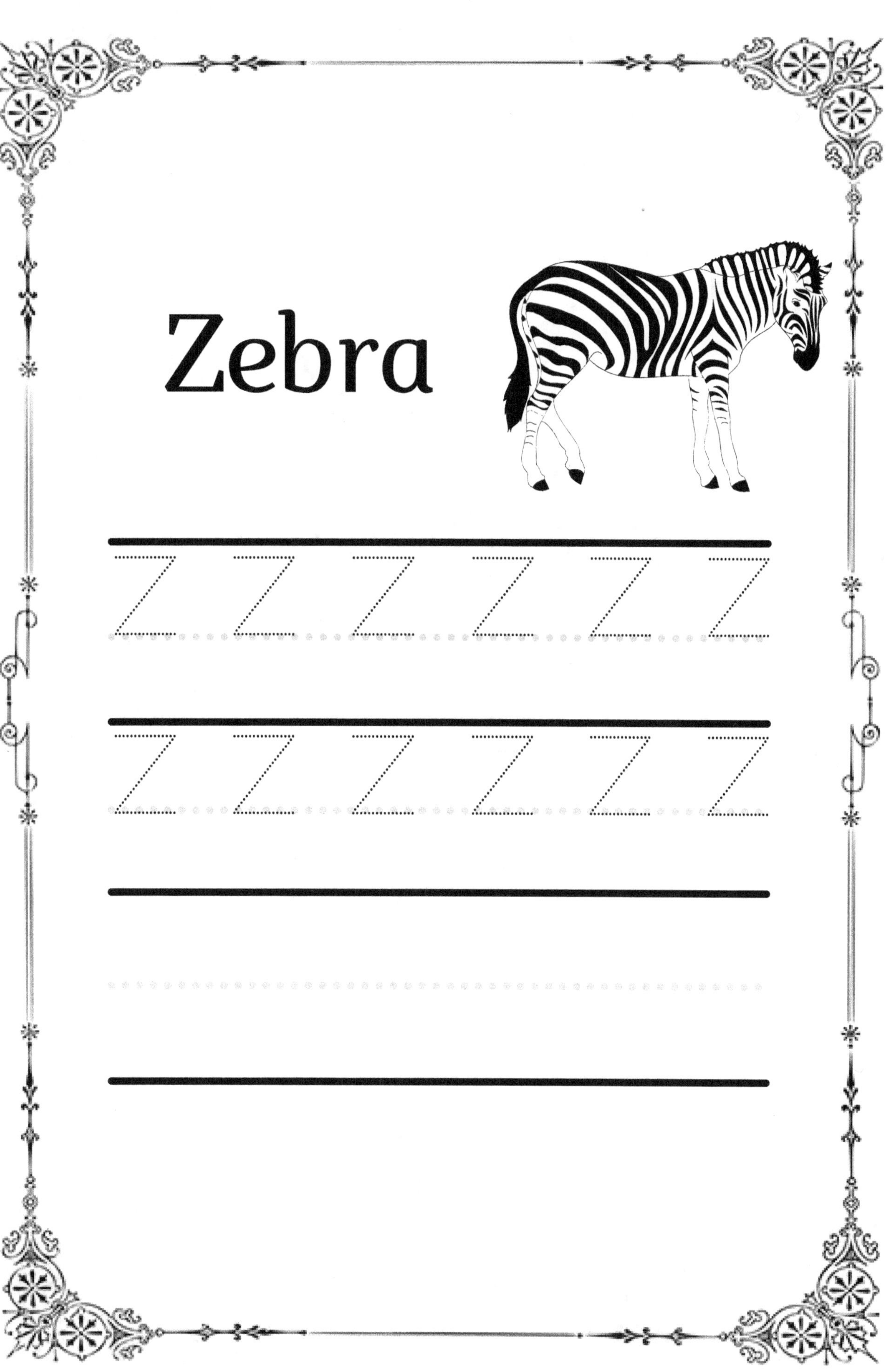

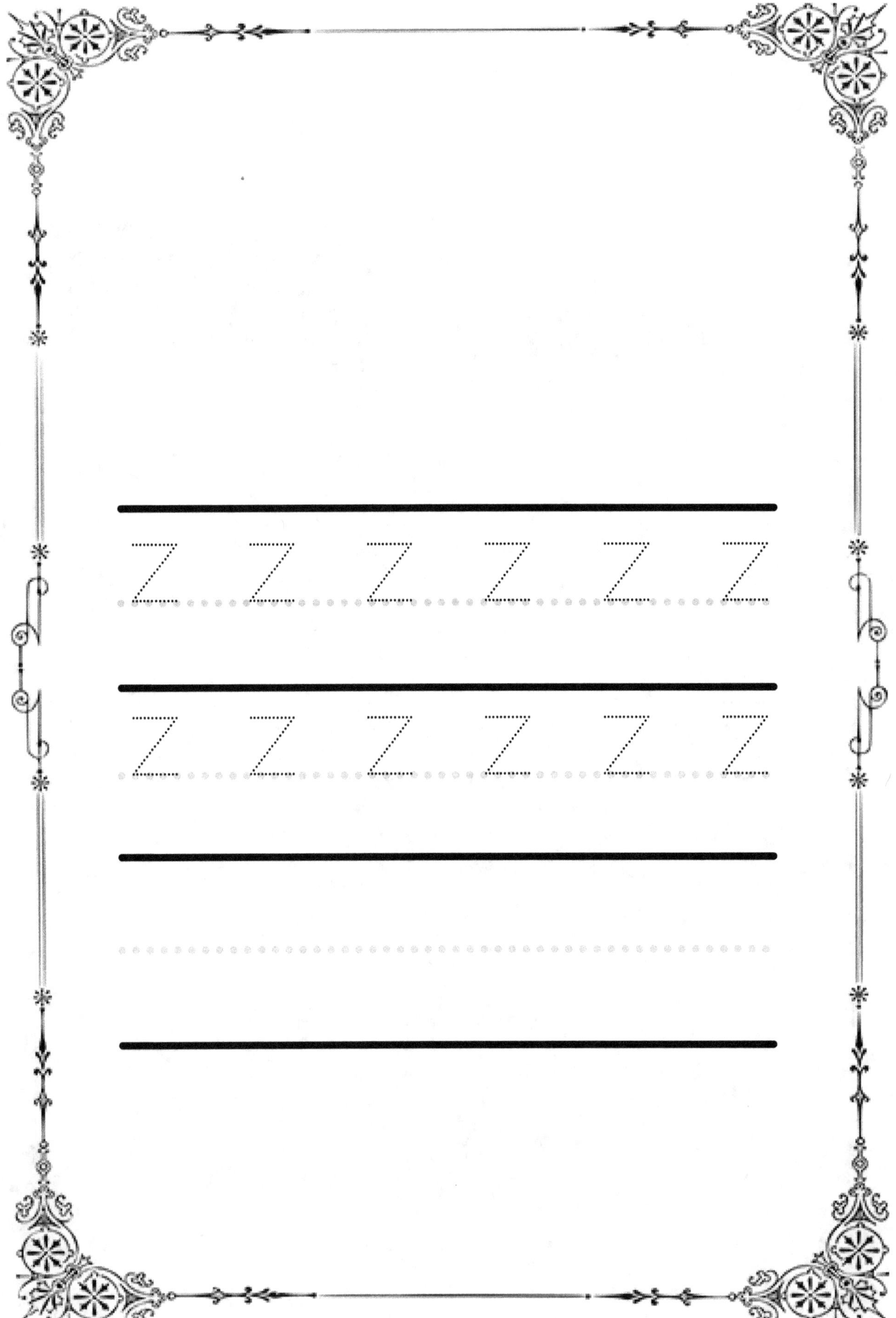

Z Z Z Z Z Z
Z Z Z Z Z Z

You have
finished the
book

Now let's have
a little fun

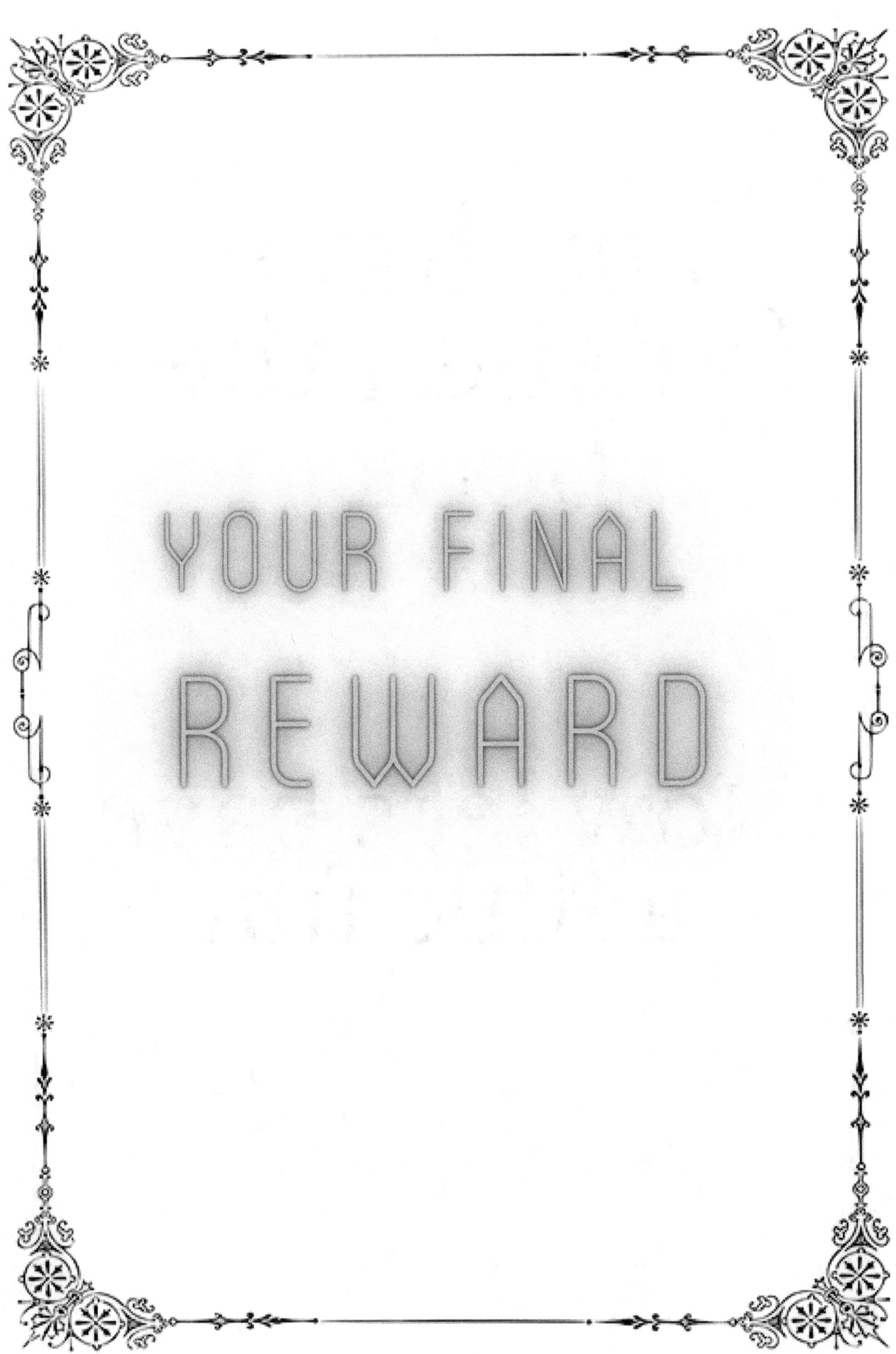

YOUR FINAL
REWARD

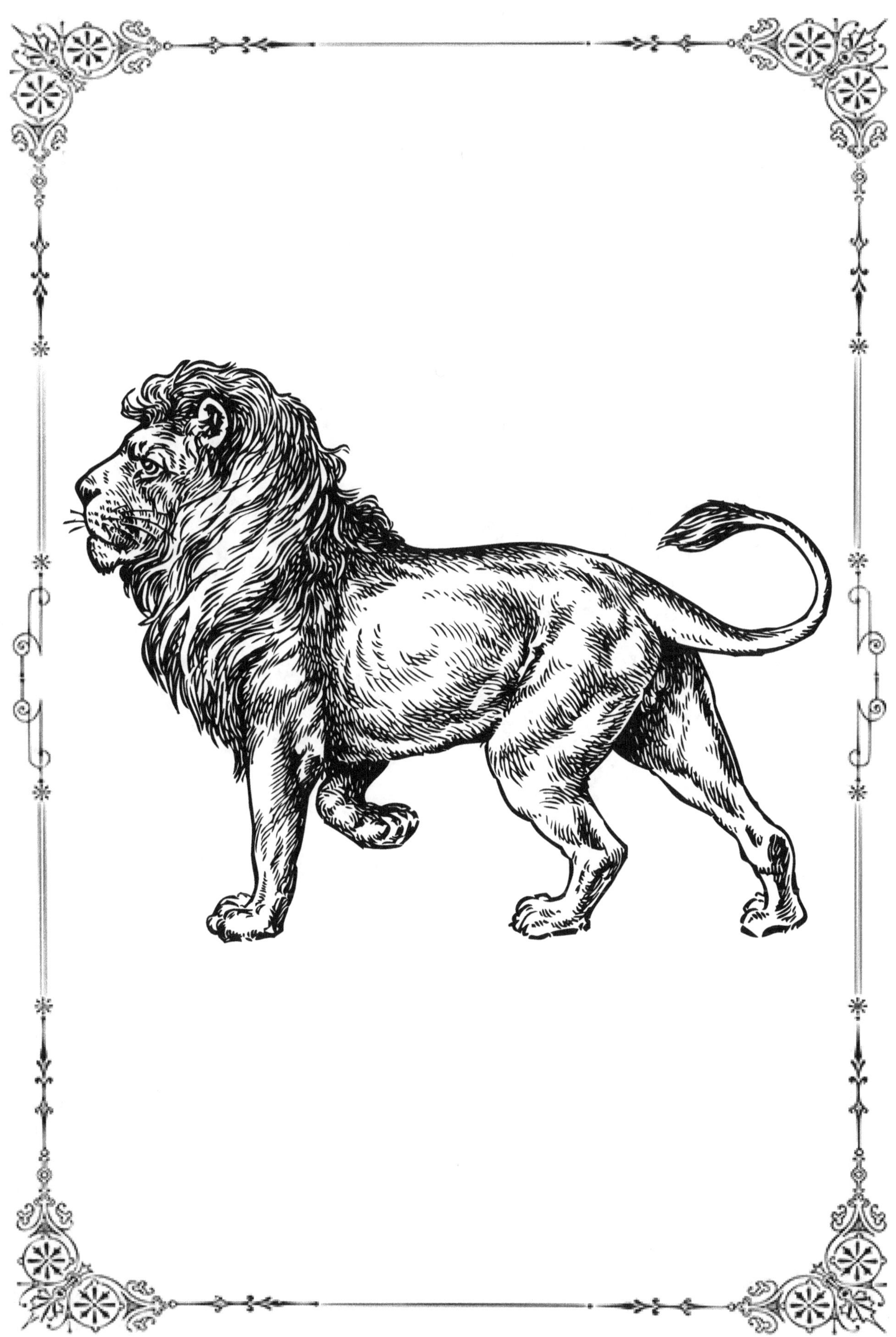

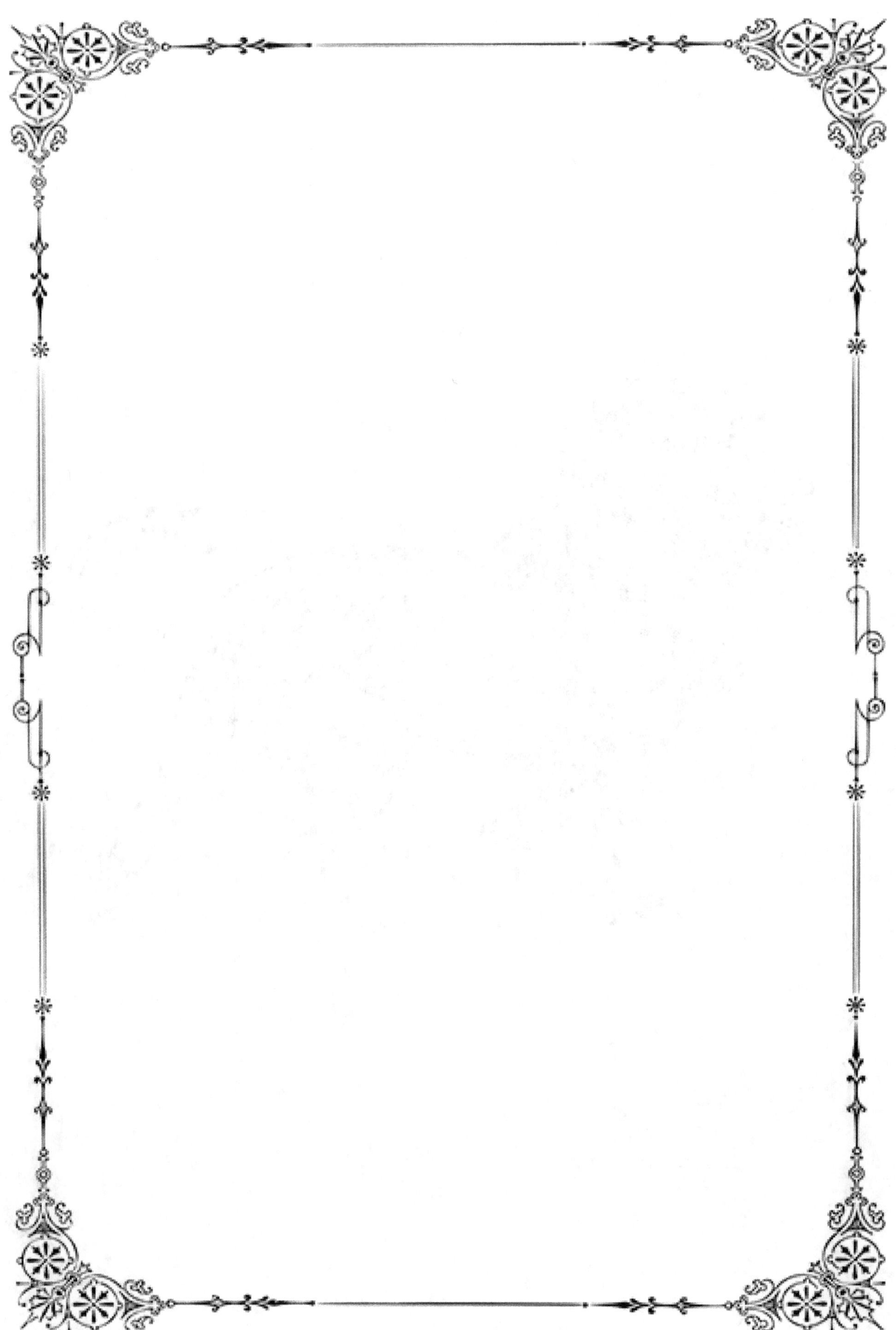

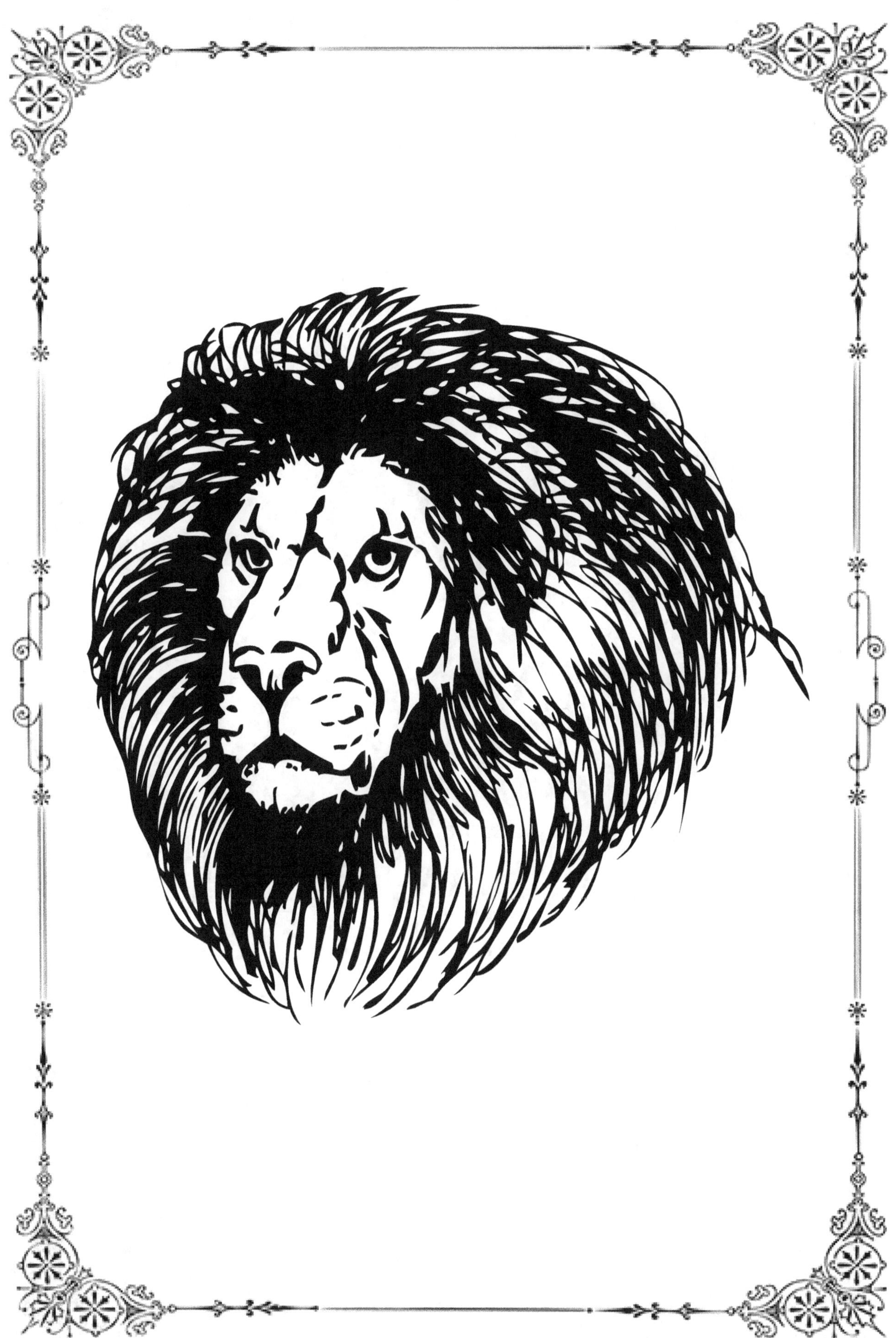

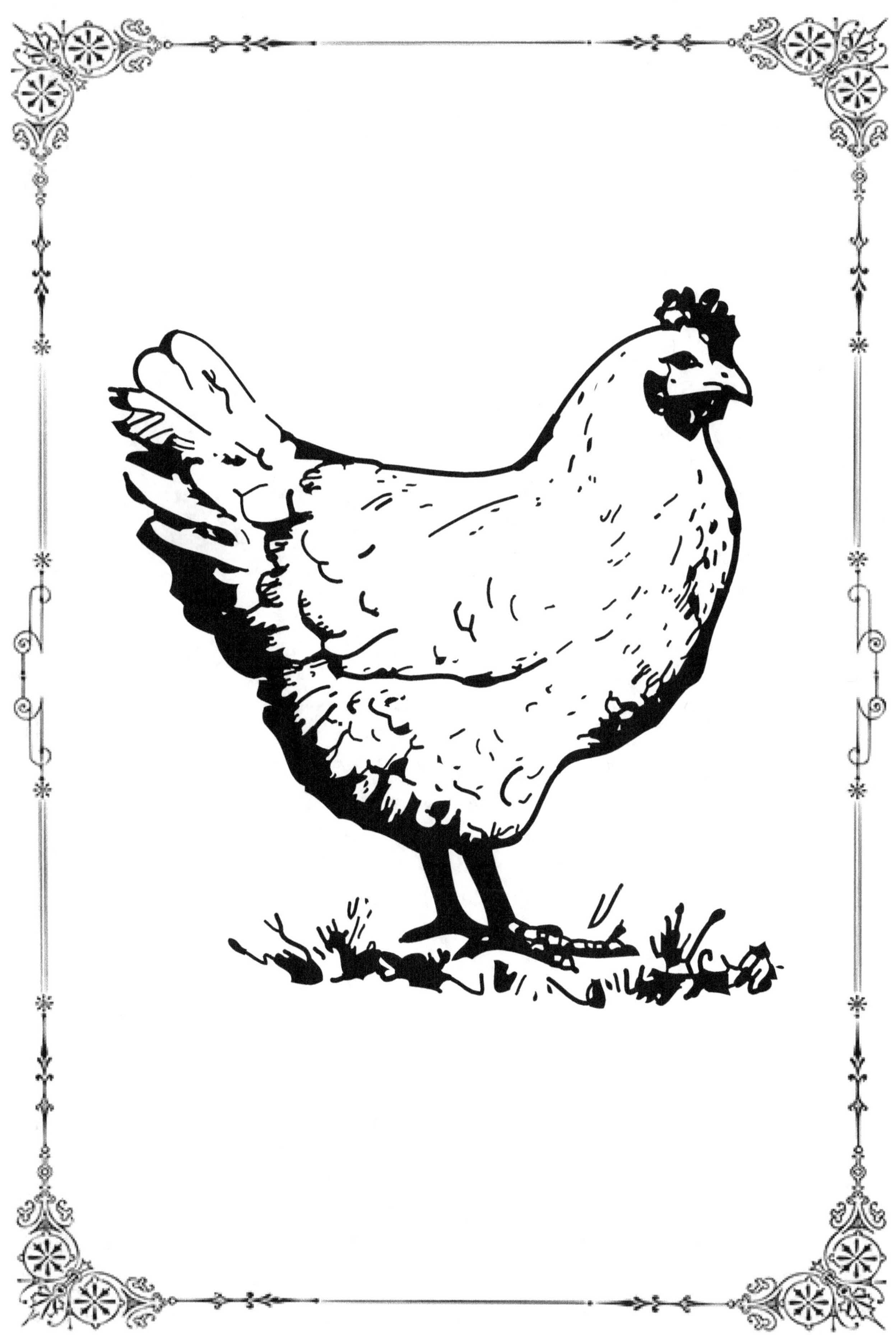

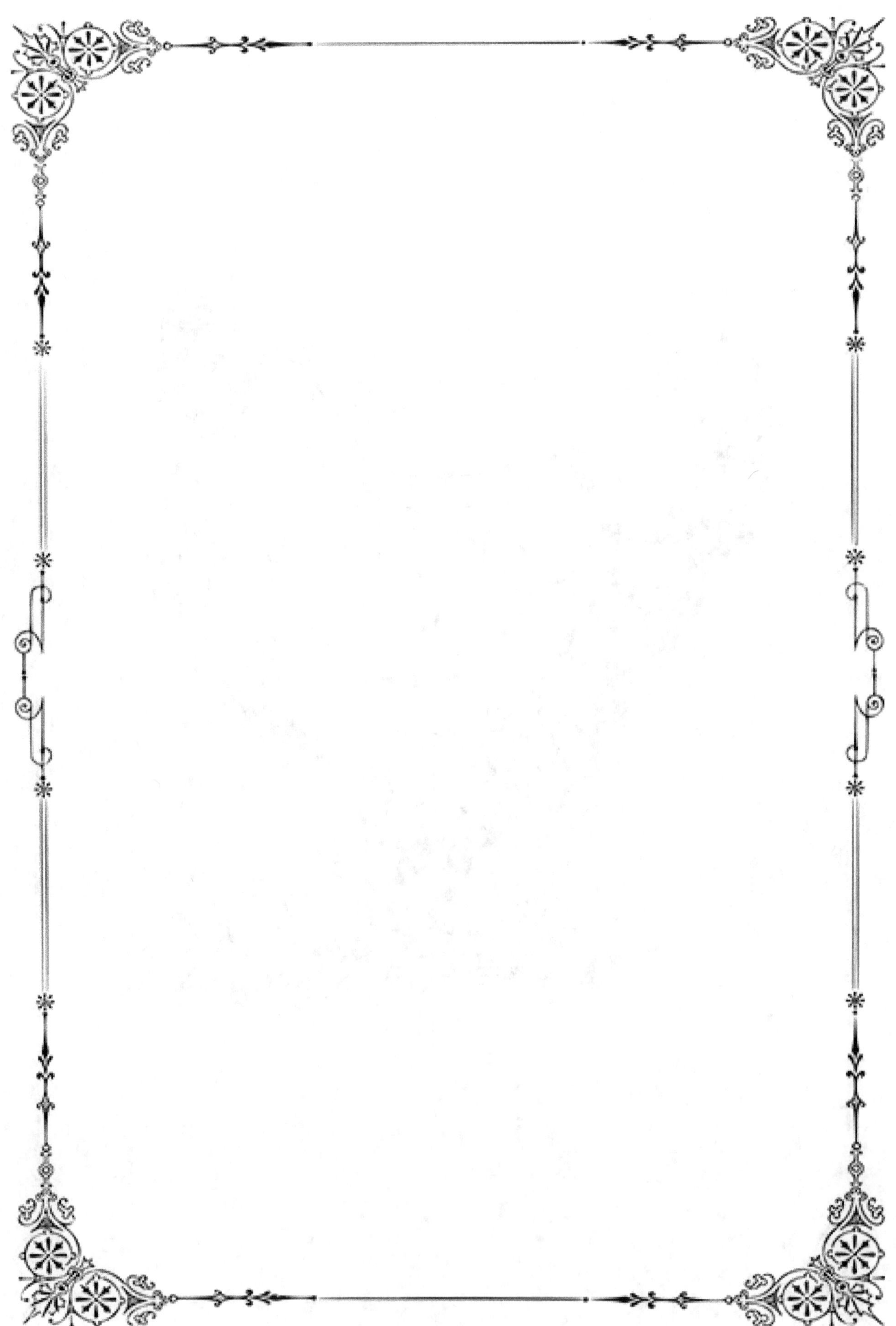

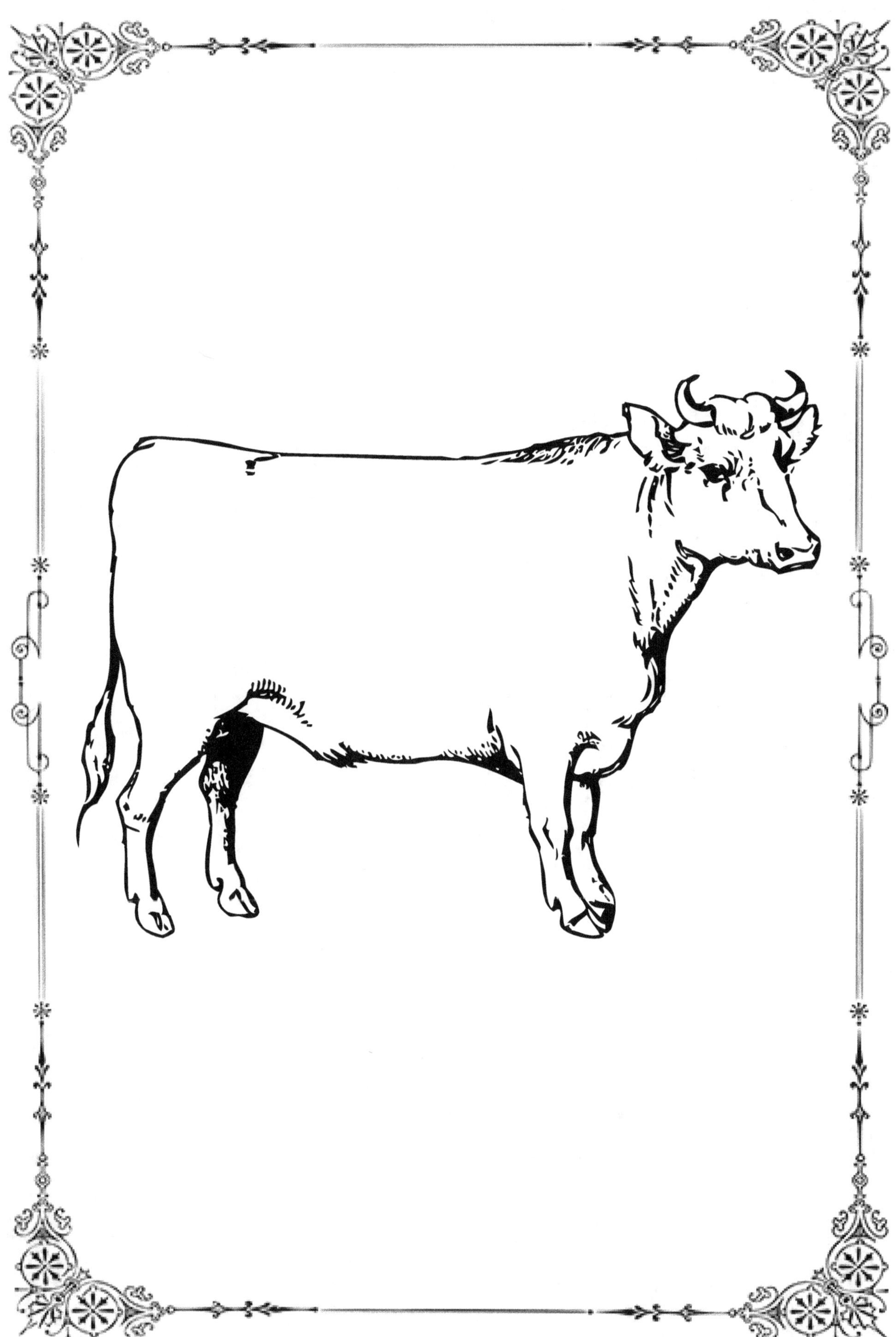

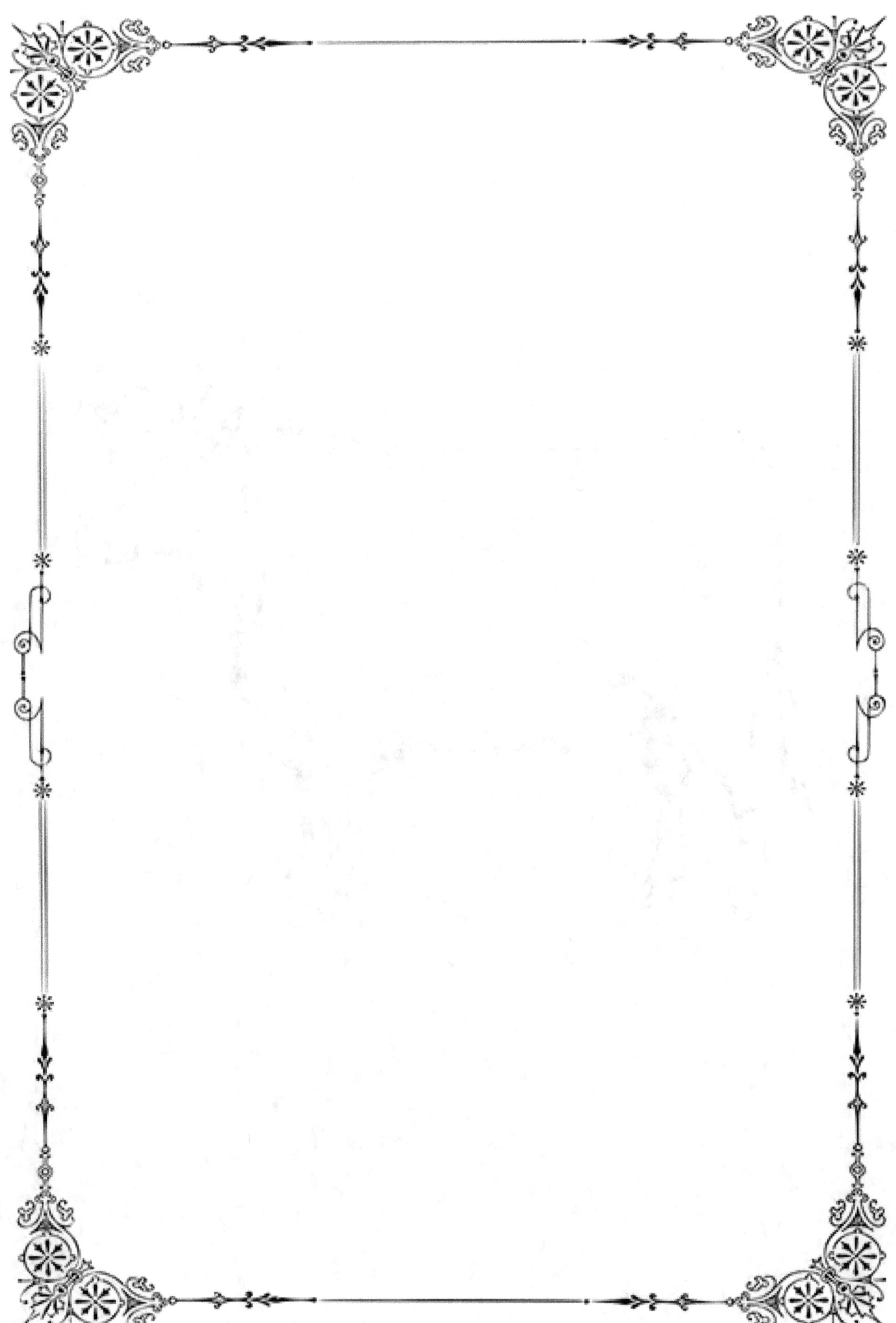

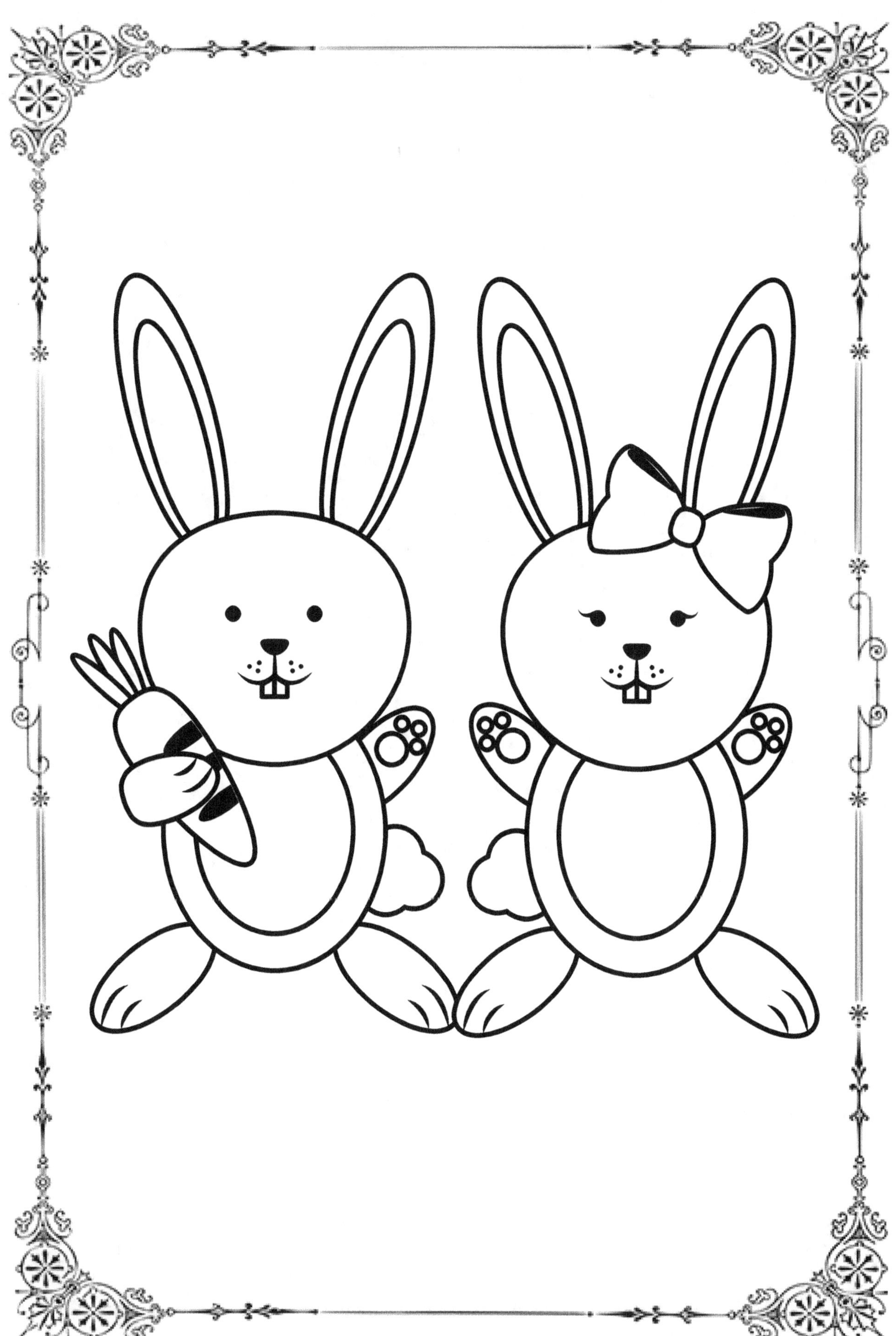

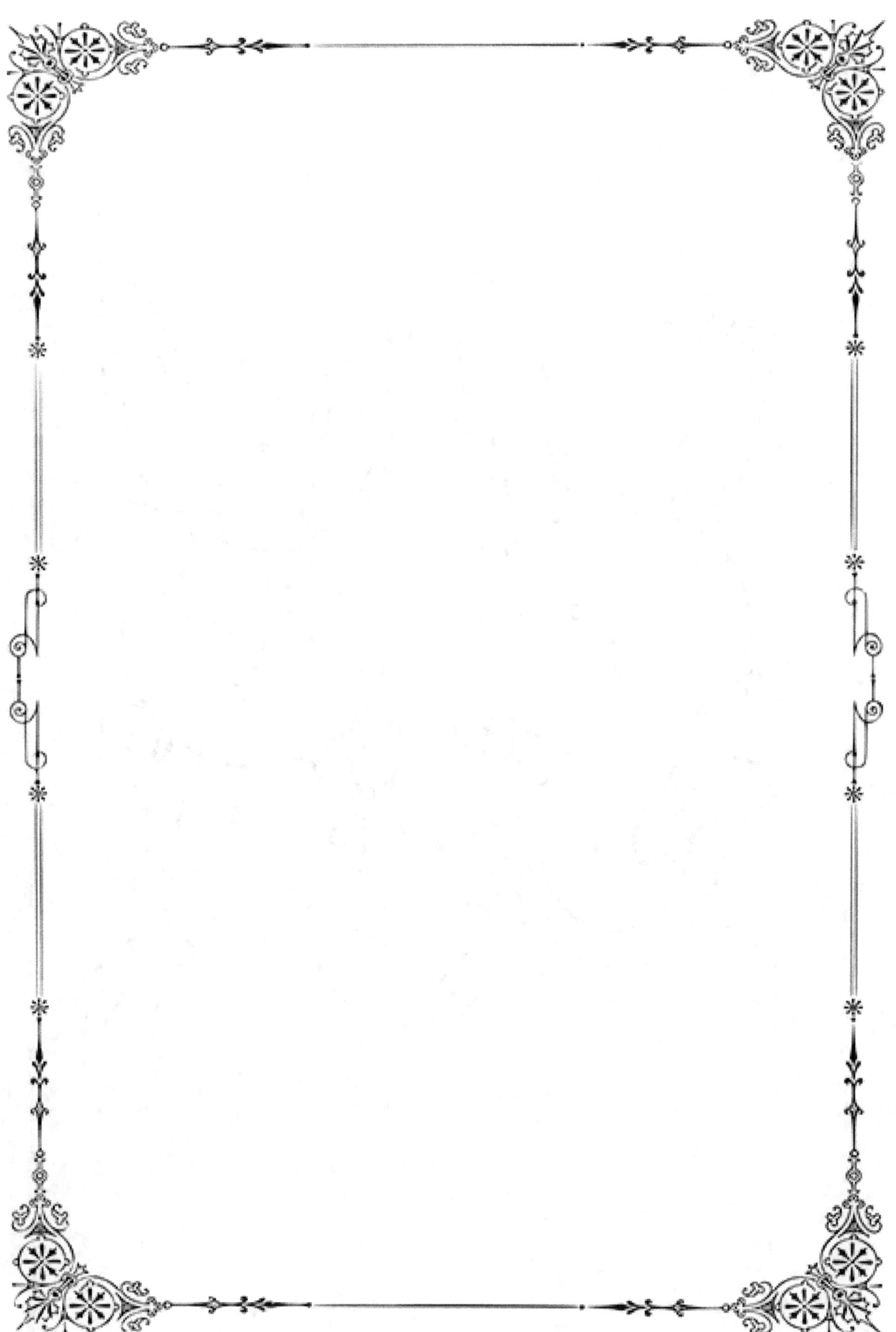

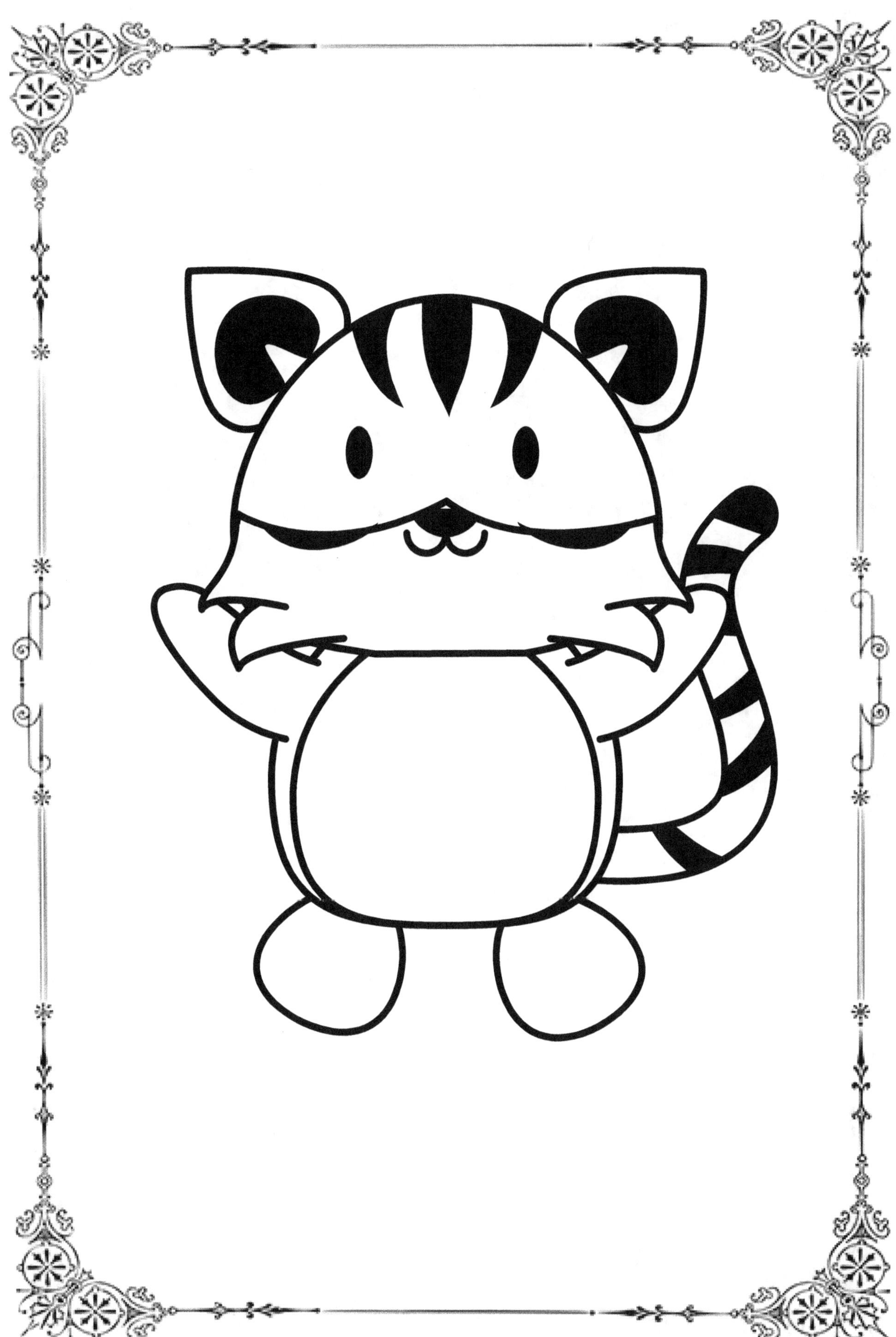

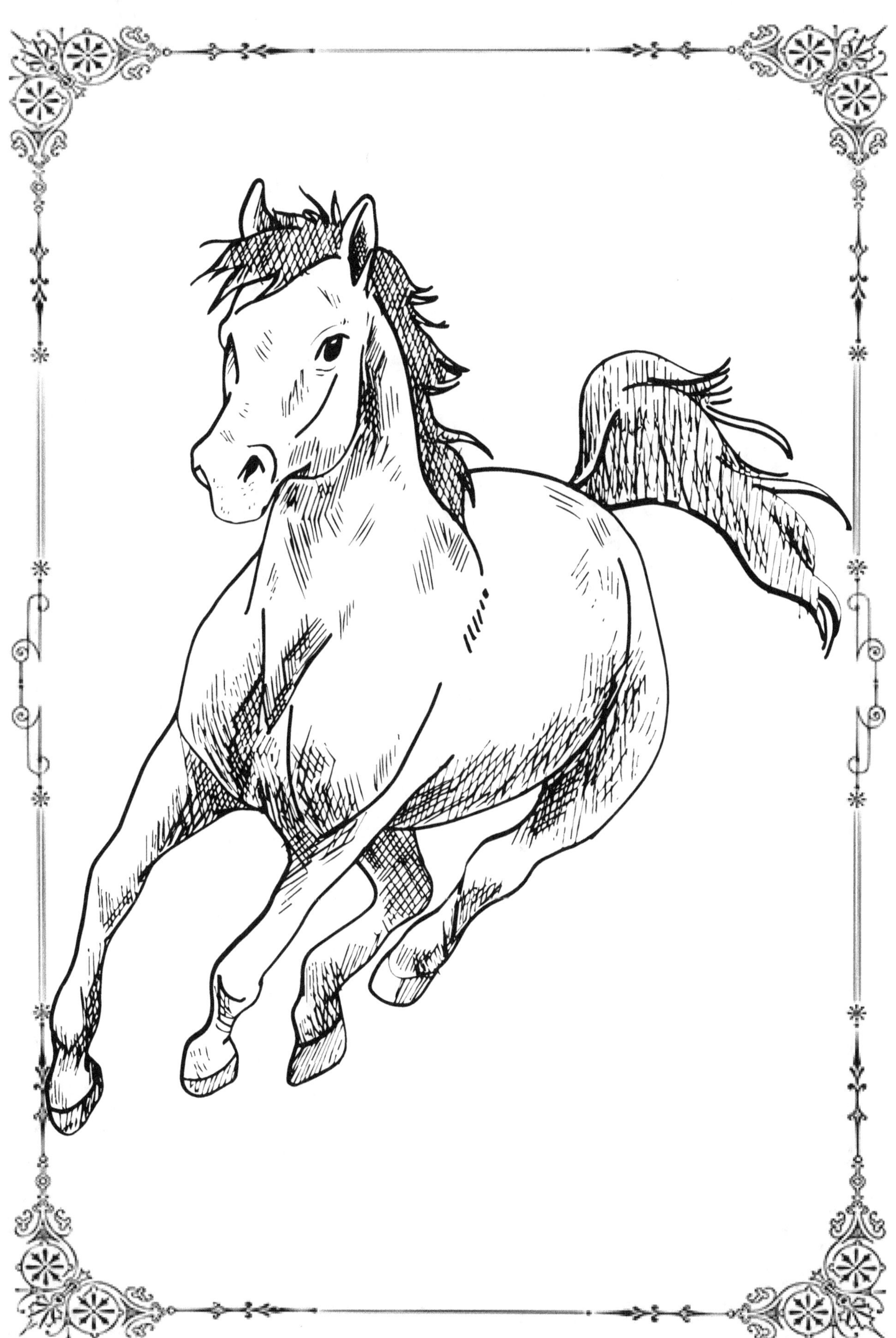

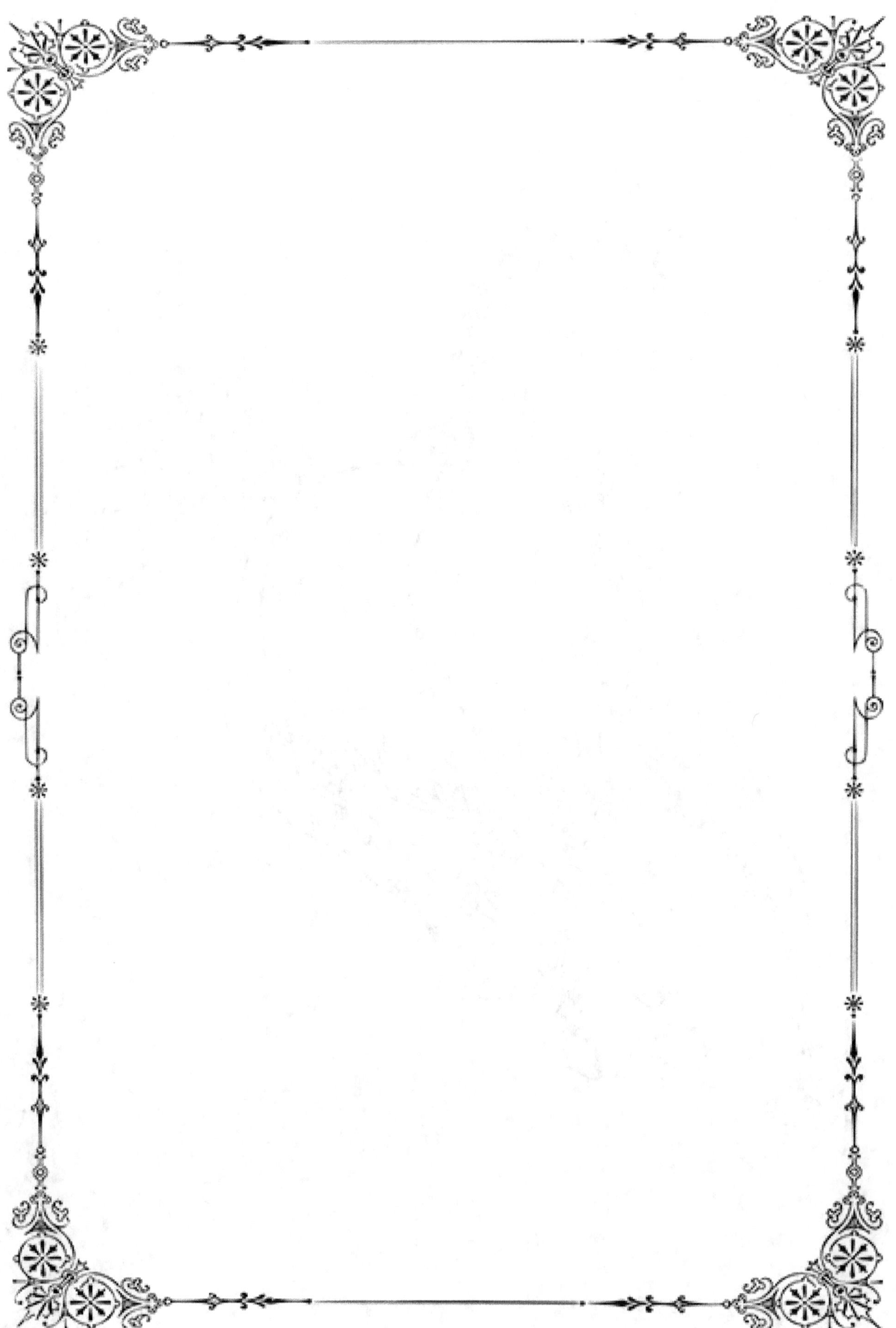

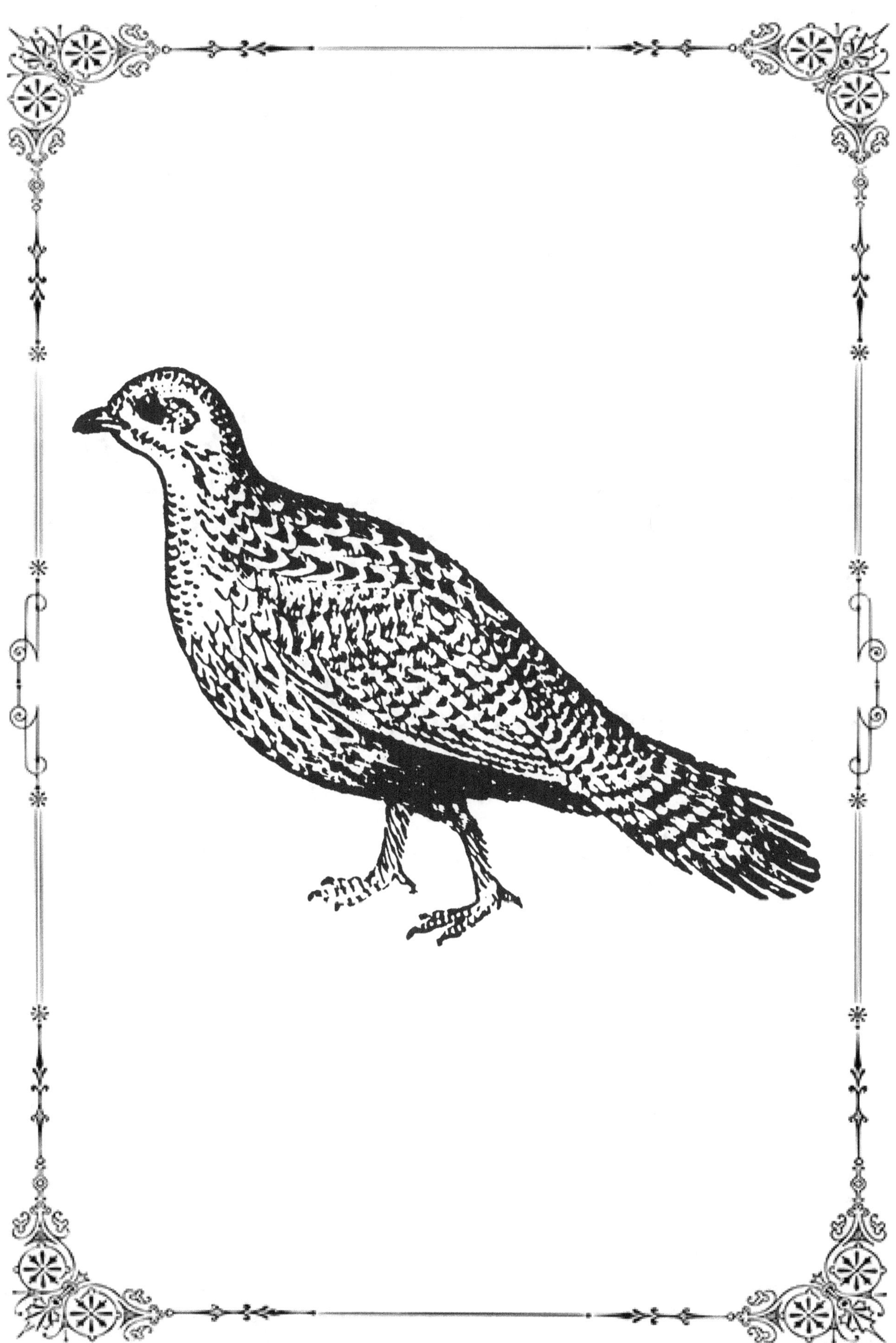